Praise for *The Checklist B*

"As a lifelong list-freak, I was ecstatic to read this book! And it does not disappoint. I've admired Alexandra's writing for years. *The Checklist Book* feels like getting a behind-the-scenes tour of her brain, seeing how she organizes her life, business, writing projects, self-care, travel, family time, and more, and how you can do it, too. Whether you're a list-fanatic (like me), list-curious, or list-phobic, you'll gain something valuable from this book."

—Theresa Reed, author of *The Tarot Coloring Book*, tarot card reader and astrologer (thetarotlady.com)

"I run a dance, voice, and acting theater training school for students, ages ten to twenty-one. Once a year, our students fly to New York City for our annual summer program. I asked Alexandra to make checklists to help the kids get prepared for the NYC trip. These checklists were such a tremendous help—helping students feel calmer and more organized, with a positive, empowered, ready-to-learn mindset. Their parents were amazed, too! One mom told me, 'I don't know *what* is going on with these checklists, but my daughter's room has never been cleaner. She's making her bed for the first time.' And now with this book, lucky reader, you get to the experience Alexandra's checklist magic for yourself!"

   —Robert Hartwell, Founder and Artistic Director, The Broadway
      Collective (bwaycollective.com)

"I haven't plowed through a book like this in forever. This is the best thing ever. Pure checklist magic! I've been so productive the last twenty-four hours. I want to buy ten thousand copies of this book and hand them out to everyone I pass on the street."

   —Gary Cassera, canine behavior specialist, founder of The
      Dog's Side (thedogsside.com) and SoulMutt dog adoption
      nonprofit (soulmutt.org)

"There are thousands of books on how to become more organized and productive, but very few have the heart, soul, humor, and gentle encouragement of this book. *The Checklist Book* is imbued with Alexandra's spirit. Emotional and practical. Visionary and realistic. She invites you to consider life's biggest questions: How do you want to live? What type of person do you aspire to be—while keeping things simple and doable? I love this book. A must-read for anyone who wishes life could feel a little calmer, simpler, and more beautiful every day."

—Ellen Fondiler, career and business strategist (ellenfondiler. com) and founder of the MEarth environmental sustainability education program (mearthcarmel.org)

Praise for Franzen's previous books

"*You're Going to Survive* is your new best friend on a bad day. Keep it by your bedside table, in your dashboard, in your purse or in your freezer next to a big pint of ice cream. Alexandra will always be there to tell you that you can do it, you must keep going, and you are meant for greatness."

> —Vanessa Van Edwards, bestselling author of *Captivate: The Science of Succeeding with People* (scienceofpeople.com)

"*You're Going To Survive* is a must-read book for anyone with an ambitious career dream. Alexandra's writing is encouraging, comforting, and uplifting, with just the right amount of get-up-and-do-it motivation."

> —Liz Dennery Sanders, brand consultant, creative director, founder of SheBrand (shebrand.com)

"Alexandra Franzen is like a cool big sister who's got your back with the kind of humor and honesty that will make you feel less alone and motivated to keep going when chasing your dream gets tough (we're talking client-from-hell, one-star-review, oh-shit-what-am-I-even-doing tough). Every creative needs *You're Going to Survive* on their nightstand for those inevitable bad days."

> —Kathleen Shannon, host of the *Being Boss* Podcast (beingboss. club) and co-founder of Braid Creative (braidcreative.com)

"A writer, a teacher, a guide, a muse: whatever Alexandra Franzen does, she does it with a mission of kindness, love, and acceptance. I don't think anyone could better navigate the lowest lows with such wisdom, humor and strength. For a book like *You're Going to Survive*, there's nobody else I'd want as my survival skills guide."

> —Michelle Ward, career coach, as seen in *New York Magazine*, *The Huffington Post*, *Newsweek* (whenigrowupcoach.com)

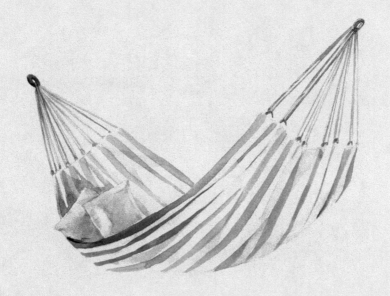

The
Checklist
Book

The Checklist Book

SET REALISTIC GOALS,
CELEBRATE TINY WINS,
REDUCE STRESS AND OVERWHELM,
AND FEEL CALMER EVERY DAY

Alexandra Franzen

TURNER
PUBLISHING COMPANY

TMA Press
An imprint of Turner Publishing Company
Nashville, Tennessee
www.turnerpublishing.com

Cover, Layout & Design: Morgane Leoni

The Checklist Book: Set Realistic Goals, Celebrate Tiny Wins, Reduce Stress and Overwhelm, and Feel Calmer Every Day

Library of Congress Cataloging-in-Publication number: 2019948628
ISBN: (print) 978-1-64250-118-6, (ebook) 978-1-64250-119-3
BISAC: SEL035000—SELF-HELP / Self-Management / Time Management

Printed in the United States of America.

HAVE YOU EVER GAZED UP INTO THE HEAVENS AND THOUGHT, "WHY AM I HERE? WHAT HAPPENS AFTER WE DIE? WHAT IS THE MEANING OF LIFE? HOW SHOULD I SPEND MY PRECIOUS TIME?"

ME TOO.

HAVE YOU EVER GLANCED AT YOUR TO-DO LIST AND THOUGHT, "OH MY GOD. I'M SO OVERWHELMED. SO DISORGANIZED. TOO MUCH TO DO. I FEEL LIKE I'M DROWNING."

ME TOO.

THIS IS THE GREAT COMEDY OF HUMAN LIFE. HERE YOU ARE, TRYING TO FIGURE OUT HOW TO RIDE THIS EARTH-SHIP THAT'S HURTLING THROUGH SPACE, CONNECT WITH POWERS GREATER THAN YOURSELF, AND MAKE MEANING OUT OF THE MYSTERY. AND AT THE SAME TIME, YOU'RE TRYING TO FIGURE OUT HOW TO ANSWER ALL OF THOSE EMAILS, EAT MORE KALE, HIT THE GYM CONSISTENTLY, PAY OFF THOSE LOANS, AND REMEMBER TO PICK UP LAUNDRY DETERGENT ON THE WAY HOME.

THE BIG, COSMIC STUFF.

THE SMALL, DAILY-LIFE STUFF.

HOW CAN WE HOLD BOTH IN OUR FEEBLE HUMAN BRAINS AT THE SAME TIME?

HOW CAN WE PLAN A DAY THAT SOMEHOW INCLUDES ROOM FOR BOTH/ALL/AND?

HOW CAN WE FEEL CALM, SECURE, FOCUSED, GROUNDED, ORGANIZED, AND PRODUCTIVE WHILE LIVING IN A UNIVERSE THAT'S SO MYSTERIOUS, SO UNFATHOMABLE, AND AT TIMES, SO PAINFUL AND CHAOTIC?

THIS BOOK IS MY ATTEMPT AT ANSWERING THESE QUESTIONS.

THE CHECKLIST BOOK IS, AS THE NAME SUGGESTS, A BOOK ABOUT HOW TO MAKE CHECKLISTS TO ORGANIZE YOUR DAY, YOUR YEAR, AND VARIOUS PROJECTS AND GOALS. BUT BEYOND THAT, THIS IS A BOOK ABOUT HOW TO CREATE A LIFE YOU CAN BE PROUD OF. A LIFE THAT FEELS DEEP AND MEANINGFUL. A LIFE THAT CULMINATES WITH YOU DYING PEACEFULLY, CONTENT, AT EASE...HOPEFULLY AT A VERY OLD AGE, AND HOPEFULLY WITH VERY FEW REGRETS.

THANK YOU FOR OPENING THIS BOOK.

WHOEVER YOU ARE, WHEREVER YOU ARE, THIS BOOK IS DEDICATED TO YOU.

Contents

FOREWORD

BY DR. SASHA HEINZ, PHD

How can we lead happy, healthy, flourishing lives?

As a psychologist, I've spent decades pondering, studying, researching, and unraveling this question.

While earning my Bachelor of Arts, Masters in Applied Positive Psychology, and PhD in Developmental Psychology (ding ding, hello, overachiever-nerd-alert!) at Harvard, University of Pennsylvania, and Columbia, I had the opportunity to learn from some of the top minds in the field—Dr. Martin Seligman, Dr. Barbara Fredrickson, and others. In my private practice, I've worked with hundreds of clients—hearing their innermost struggles, private fears, triumphs and victories.

So, okay then, what's the deal? What's the key to having a life that feels satisfying, beautiful, and meaningful? Is it about financial security—having five, six, seven, or eight digits in your bank account? Is it about your physical health and physique—having toned abs and the ability to run an eight-minute mile? Is it faith—belief in a higher power? Prayer? Meditation? Community? A happy marriage and family life? A career that you love? Some/all of the above? The answer is: it depends. No two people are exactly alike. We all have different values that determine what "a good life" looks and feels like.

However, research indicates that there's one thing that virtually all human beings share in common, which is a desire for *integrity*.

We all want to feel proud of ourselves. We all want to feel like we can trust ourselves. We all want to honor the commitments we've made rather than flaking out. We all want to make promises to ourselves—and others—and actually keep the promises we've made.

There's something universally satisfying about making a list of meaningful goals/intentions/promises, checking things off, and basking in the golden glow of accomplishment. As humans, we love that sweet feeling of alignment, solidity, and integrity: "I said I would do it. I did it. I followed through. It's done."

Research shows, the more promises you keep, the better you feel. There's a direct connection between your level of personal integrity (promises kept, boxes checked, intentions fulfilled) and your self-esteem, happiness, and wellbeing.

The Checklist Book is your invitation to gently assess your life. How are you living? What kind of promises are you making and why? Which kinds of goals matter to you and which don't? What belongs on your checklist for today and what doesn't? What does "a good life" mean to you?

I've had the pleasure of working with Alexandra on several projects—including a book proposal, articles, workbooks, self-assessments, and other materials for my clients. Alex is a gifted writer, prolific artist and entrepreneur, a wonderfully dorky nerd-ball (this is a compliment!) with a house full of checklists and bulletin boards, and someone who just intuitively "gets" how human brains work, and what people need to thrive and succeed.

She's encouraging and tender—the type of person who records a three-minute audio message and emails it to you before bedtime just to remind you: "You're doing a great job." She's a little bit like Fred Rogers except with blue hair and yoga pants. You're in good hands with her. Enjoy this book. Happy list-making. Enjoy the journey of raising your level of integrity—closing the gap between the life you wish to lead, and the life you're actually living.

Dr. Sasha Heinz, PhD
Sun Valley, Idaho, 2019

INTRODUCTION

Take What You Need

Once upon a time, I attended a mixed-level yoga class in Portland, Oregon led by my friend Justin. At the beginning of class, as we unrolled our mats and settled into the room, Justin smiled and told us:

"During this class, please know that everything I say is simply a *suggestion*. Not a rigid command that you must follow. Just a suggestion. If there's a particular pose that feels really good for you, wonderful, stay in it and enjoy it. If there's a particular pose that doesn't feel good for you, then don't do it. If there's a pose that you want to modify in some way, go for it. Nothing is mandatory. Do what feels right for you. The whole point of this class is for you to leave feeling *better* than when you arrived. So, please take what you need and leave the rest."

As you read this book, I invite you to adopt the same attitude. Everything I describe in this book—including how to make a Daily Checklist, Seasonal Checklist, Survival Checklist, Workout Checklist, etc.—is simply a suggestion. If something intrigues you, try it. If something doesn't resonate with you, skip it.

Take what you need and leave the rest.

ALEX

CHAPTER ONE

The Power of Making
a Checklist

A TRUE STORY ABOUT ME, MY YOUNGER

SISTER, AND THE POWERFUL ACT OF MAKING A

CHECKLIST. HOW MY LIFELONG OBSESSION WITH

CHECKLISTS—AND MY PERSONAL METHOD FOR

MAKING CHECKLISTS—CAME INTO BEING.

It was two days before the beginning of a brand new year. I came home from the grocery store to find my beautiful, brilliant sister... sobbing and clutching fistfuls of tissue, huddled in a damp snot-puddle on the floor.

Olivia, my younger sibling, was twenty-seven years old at the time. I found her slumped in my living room with her suitcase open, belongings strewn all around, staring down at the carpeting.

She'd been visiting for the winter holidays and spent the last few weeks with me. I was excited to have her in town and eager to show her my new life in Hilo—a small, quirky, coastal city in Hawaii where I'd moved just a few months prior.

For the last fourteen days, I'd proudly presented the pineapples growing in my backyard, my favorite swimming hole, the best ahi poke on the planet, a majestic green sand beach. I took Olivia hither and yon, down red dirt roads, through jungle trails, all over the island, determined to give her the best vacation of all time. (And, you know, hopefully earn the official title of Coolest Big Sister Ever.)

Olivia was sweet and affectionate as always, linking her arm with mine as we walked and talked, laughing when I told our favorite inside-jokes ("Crack a window!" "Welcome to paperclip village!"). And yet, at many points during her visit, an invisible cloud seemed to hang over my sister's head. She seemed somewhat distant, distracted, and tightly wound. She'd get strangely agitated over tiny mistakes that wouldn't ordinarily bother her in the slightest—like accidentally tossing a hand-wash-only top into the machine.

I didn't pry for information, but I could sense that my sister was tense and preoccupied for some reason—perhaps *many* reasons. A heavy load of emotional weight rested on her shoulders.

I know that feeling all too well.

Even when your physical body is in paradise—rainbows, sunshine, coconuts, and palm trees all around—your mind can be one thousand miles away, ruminating on difficult, worrisome things.

Finally, on the last day of her visit, as she was packing up for her flight back home, everything came bubbling to the surface. Like the Kilauea Volcano that had erupted earlier that same year— spewing up thick, viscous lava—my sister's troubles poured out.

"I just..." Olivia burbled, amidst tears. "I just...feel so overwhelmed."

"About what?" I asked, setting down the groceries and coming to her side.

"EVERYTHING," she moaned.

I flopped onto the floor beside her.

"Okay," I said. "What kind of 'everything'? Do you want to talk about it?"

She did.

What Olivia described felt so achingly familiar to me because it's something I've experienced so many times in my life. A situation that, I'm guessing, you've experienced too. A situation that can be summarized in ten words:

TOO MUCH TO DO.
NOT ENOUGH HOURS IN THE DAY.

Over the next hour, Olivia shared everything that had been weighing heavily on her spirit. It all came out in a tumble. Parts of the story I knew, others I did not.

Olivia was attending graduate school full-time, working towards her master's degree and earning straight A's in all of her classes. This program was incredibly rewarding—and also, incredibly expensive. She was (understandably) nervous about racking up student loan debt that she'd never be able to repay. This anxiety crept around her neck, hot and itchy, invading her dreams, often keeping her awake at night.

To earn money, she'd gotten a part-time job and was working as many hours as she could. But this still wasn't enough to cover the high cost of living in Boulder, Colorado. To reduce her expenses, she had found a unique living situation. She had her own private room in a lovely house—completely free—in exchange for doing yard work, dog walking, snow shoveling, and various other errands for the owner, Olivia's godmother, who lived onsite.

It was great to save money on rent, but in between going to lectures at school, studying for exams, writing papers, working a job, and dealing with the housing-work-trade-barter situation and lengthy commutes up and down treacherous, snowy mountain roads, Olivia had virtually zero free time. Her days were crammed from dawn until bedtime.

On top of all this, her heart had been trampled by a romantic relationship that had turned sour a few months ago. Grieving this breakup made handling "the rest of life" even more difficult. Additional stress on top of stress.

She wanted to excel at school and graduate with honors. She wanted to earn enough money to cover her expenses without strain. She wanted to stay connected with friends and family, not let these relationships wither due to her busy schedule. She also wanted time to take care of her body—time to practice yoga, time to meditate, time to cook nutritious meals, and time to rest and sleep (what a concept!).

Eventually, she also wanted to meet a wonderful man, fall in love, buy some land, plant a garden, start a family, and raise children together. Her dreams were not exactly unusual or extravagant— we're not talking about gold-plated toilets on a diamond-encrusted yacht—and yet, in this moment on my living room floor, everything felt so hard to reach. Life was so busy. Money was so tight. Time was so limited. Everything just felt so...overwhelming.

I could hear the pain in her voice, the spoken questions, and the unspoken ones, too. *How will I care for a child if I can barely take care of myself? How will I get from here to where I long to be? How is it possible that I'm a smart, grown-up, adult person, and yet I'm still struggling with the most basic things—like figuring out how to manage my time?*

"I always have so much to do. I never have enough time for everything. I feel like I'm drowning," she finished bluntly, tears gushing from her eyes.

And so, here was Olivia's predicament. A familiar dilemma, painfully relatable for me, and for so many people. *Too much to do. Not enough hours in the day. Competing priorities. Overwhelm. Fried nerves.*

New Year's Eve was forty-eight hours away. But rather than feeling optimistic about the year ahead, Olivia already felt exhausted and anxious about everything that needed to be done. And the year hadn't even begun.

"You've got a lot on your plate—and a lot on your mind," I said. "It's totally understandable that you feel overwhelmed."

I hate seeing my sister (or anyone, really) in pain. I wish I could wave a magic wand and instantly erase all of my sister's worries and struggles. I couldn't offer a magic wand—but I could offer something else. Something to create a little more calm amidst the mental chaos.

"Do you want to try something with me?" I asked.

"What?" she sniffled.

"Let's make a checklist."

FROM MENTAL CHAOS BACK TO CALM.

I gave Olivia a hug. We made a pot of ginger tea with honey. I brought out some big sheets of paper, Sharpie markers, bulletin boards, and brass tacks. We sat cross-legged and hashed it all out.

We started with some basic questions:

- What are your biggest priorities for the next season?
- What are your tiny goals for today? Tomorrow? The next day?
- Okay, how many of those goals can you *realistically* complete in a single day, while still leaving space for showering, eating, sleeping—you know, basic human-body maintenance?
- Have you been over-extending yourself, tying to cram an unreasonable number of activities into each day?
- If so, how could we scale things back to a more humane, manageable level?

About an hour later, we had distilled the maelstrom in her mind into a couple of neat, orderly checklists.

First, a *Seasonal Checklist*. A checklist of her biggest priorities for the next three months. The big things she wanted to accomplish and experience over the next ninety days.

Second, a *Loose-End Checklist*. A checklist of all the random, miscellaneous loose ends that she wanted to tie up. Little bits and bobs that had been floating around in her mind like old pennies, gum wrappers, and lint at the bottom of a backpack, creating that uneasy "I know I must be forgetting something..." feeling.

Third, a *Daily Checklist*. A checklist for tomorrow—not the whole week, just the next day—so she could get a good night's sleep, wake up refreshed, and have a clear plan for the day ahead— already printed and laid out in advance.

Her tears dried. Her shoulders dropped out of her ears. The storm clouds seemed to be parting.

"Feel better?" I asked.

She did.

Significantly better.

All because of one hour of talking and planning, a few sheets of paper, a pen. Nothing flashy or complicated. Just making a few lists, which is something that most people instinctively know how to do.

I could see the glow of hope returning to Olivia's eyes. She still had a very demanding year ahead—no doubt—but after one hour of checklist-making, she seemed at least 20 percent more confident in her abilities to handle things successfully. Sometimes, 20 percent makes all the difference in the world.

This is why I love checklists—and why I felt inspired to write an entire book about them.

HOW CHECKLISTS HAVE CHANGED MY LIFE.

For most of my life—practically as long as I can remember—I've used checklists to organize my life. From the moment I could hold a pencil in my hands and write, I've been making lists and checking them off.

I was very young when I first experienced the oh-so-satisfying sensation of putting a big, fat checkmark next to a completed item. Even as I type that word—*checkmark*—I feel an involuntary sigh, a feeling of sweet release, an almost erotic thrill (hahahaaaaa—oh, but it's true) cascading through my body. Ahhhh. The glorious checkmark. The powerful symbol of an intention that's been set—and realized. A goal—achieved. A victory—won. Visible evidence of progress—made.

I love checklists with a fervor that delights some and frightens others. As Brenda, my editor at Mango Publishing, once put it, "Alex, once you start talking about checklists, you get this...um... *gleam* in your eyes."

I think "gleam" is a euphemism for "evangelistic, manic zeal."

Brenda is right. Once you get me talking about checklists, the gleam arises, and it's difficult for me to stop—because checklists have shaped my life in so many beautiful ways. I just want to spread the Checklist Gospel to anyone who's willing to listen.

Checklists have helped me to navigate several complex, long-distance moves—from Los Angeles to New Zealand, New Zealand to Minnesota, Minnesota to Oregon, and Oregon to Hawaii.

Checklists have made it possible for me to complete numerous professional projects with tight deadlines, even tighter budgets, and lots of moving parts—including producing events in more than twenty cities around the world, writing several books (and securing book deals), writing hundreds of articles and essays, working behind-the-scenes as a writer, editor, consultant, and content creator for my clients, launching my own website, business, and podcast, and years later, launching a book publishing imprint called The Tiny Press.

But the *biggest* reason why I love checklists—and why I felt compelled to write this book—is because checklists have helped me to strike a much healthier balance between "work" and "the rest of my life."

By making checklists, I'm able to plan my day more thoughtfully and direct my time more effectively. Armed with a simple, neat, one-page list for the day, I find it's much easier to make time for my loved ones, time for my health, time for connecting with nature, time for the experiences that really matter to me—experiences that have nothing to do with invoices, spreadsheets, or emails.

When I think back through the years of my life, my most precious, treasured moments include spontaneously booking a plane ticket to surprise my dad on Father's Day. (I will never forget the look on his face.) Snuggling in bed with my mom and rubbing her feet while we watched British TV dramas in the middle of the afternoon just because we felt like it. Making Swedish meatballs on Christmas Eve with my brother and his wife. Braiding my sister's long, dark hair while she played Dixie Chicks songs on the guitar. Driving around in my old, scuffed up baby blue Volkswagen Beetle convertible with the top rolled down and my friend Kate playing DJ. Grieving a life-shattering breakup with the man I thought was my forever-mate, sobbing, staring at the ocean, asking God for a sign, and then—as if on cue, a cosmic wink—a humpback whale leaping from the depths of the sea.

On my deathbed, these are the memories that will flash before my eyes.

Not the thousands of emails I've answered.

And *this* is why I get that wild gleam in my eyes when I talk about checklists. Because for me, checklists are not really about *doing* more. For me, checklists are about *living* more—making room in your life for the moments that matter, for the beautiful memories that you'll carry to your deathbed.

THE FRANZEN CHECKLIST METHOD.

I have a unique way of making checklists.

It's not just "writing down a bunch of stuff I need to do."

There's a particular method I've developed, which I'll teach you in the pages of this book.

This method, which for simplicity's sake I call The Franzen Checklist Method, is informed by several things:

- My lifelong practice of yoga, which taught me the importance of setting a clear intention before beginning a new project, goal, day, week, month—anything in life.
- My early-life training in music, dance, theater, and improv comedy (thousands of hours in total), which taught me the value of creatively experimenting, trusting your instincts, and improvising when something doesn't feel right.

- My helicopter pilot training in my late teens/early twenties (I'll share that story with you later!), which was my first exposure to Pre-Flight Checklists—mandatory checklists which can prevent tragic mistakes and literally save your life.

- Conversations with dozens of psychologists, counselors, and life coaches—wonderful friends, clients, and colleagues—about how the mind works, why people get stuck, and how to get unstuck.

- Years of trial and error and experimentation on myself, trying to figure out which types of checklists work best for my brain and why.

All of this has gelled together to create a particular way of approaching checklists—in particular, making a Daily Checklist, which you'll learn in chapter five of this book.

To be honest, I didn't even realize that I had a "special approach" or "unique method" until I starting teaching my checklist-making process to other people—from clients to friends and family. People told me, "This is pretty cool. You should really put your checklist method into a book or something."

At first I resisted—"Oh no, that's silly. It's not like I'm a psychologist or anything like that. This is just something I do for myself. It's no big deal"—but several people lovingly nudged and encouraged me.

My confidence grew after I decided to teach a class called "Get It Done," which had around fifty students in attendance. The students were diverse. Teenagers. College students. Professors. Full-time parents. Business owners. All ages. All the way up to people in their sixties, seventies, and beyond.

The purpose of the class was to choose a project that they had been procrastinating on—any type of project, like a creative project, business project, financial project, house/domestic project, or a personal project like writing poetry or editing a series of YouTube videos, any project they had been neglecting or avoiding—focus on their project for three days in a row, and finally get it done.

On the first day of class, I taught the Franzen Checklist Method and urged everyone to send photographic evidence to me.

"Take a photo of your checklist first thing in the morning and please email it to me," I told everyone. "Then, at the end of the day, before bedtime, take another photo of your checklist—hopefully, all filled up with checkmarks. Send that photo to me too."

Soon, my inbox was filled with people's beautiful checklists—which to me, is basically the equivalent of tantalizing X-rated pornography. I was in heaven. People emailed to report: "This is really helping me feel calmer!" "I feel organized!" "Look! I can barely believe it! I did almost everything on my list!"

Several months after the class ended, I still got occasional emails from participants saying things like, "I've become obsessed with checklists" or, "This has helped so much."

Now, years later, after sharing my checklist methods with friends, family, clients, colleagues, students, and approximately 12,000 e-newsletter readers who follow my work online, I'm so happy to teach my methods to you.

MY INTENTION FOR THIS BOOK.

I begin every creative project with an intention, much like setting an intention before meditating.

Here is my intention for *The Checklist Book*.

- Gently help you evaluate your life and make some important decisions about where your time is going.

- Teach you my personal checklist methods, which I've used for years behind-the-scenes in my own life and career—and which I've also taught to people of all ages, from high school students to CEOs.

- Help you set realistic goals, celebrate tiny wins, reduce stress and overwhelm, and feel calmer (and more proud of yourself) every day.
- Ultimately, help you die peacefully and exit this world with more memories that you cherish—and fewer regrets.
- **To help you make some checklists!**

CHECKLISTS

ARE

MAGIC

CHAPTER TWO

The History of Checklists

THE TRAGIC EVENT THAT LED TO THE WORLD'S

FIRST MODERN CHECKLIST. HOW CHECKLISTS

HAVE BEEN USED IN DIFFERENT INDUSTRIES,

INCLUDING TECHNOLOGY, HOSPITALITY, AND

MEDICINE. THE ORIGIN OF THE CLASSIC

CHECKMARK SYMBOL.

When I was nineteen, I dropped out of college and decided I would become a professional helicopter pilot.

My parents, understandably, were somewhat distressed by this sudden and unexpected change of plans.

"Really?" I recall my dad asking me. He is a kind, stoic, sensible man of few words with a strong, Swedish jawline, and the first of his bloodline to graduate from college—a privilege his immigrant parents never had. "*Really?*" Such bewilderment was layered into that two-syllable question.

My parents were mystified as to why I'd walk away from a generous undergraduate scholarship. My folks were also concerned for my physical safety. They remembered, all too vividly, that it had taken me three separate attempts (yes, *three*) to pass my vehicle driving exam a few years earlier. (During one of my doomed attempts, I hit the curb while exiting the exam parking lot—to my immense embarrassment.)

I imagine my parents were probably thinking, *Alexandra can barely operate a Toyota Corolla on flat terrain at fifteen miles an hour. Perhaps a career in aviation is not the ideal path for our daughter...* Needless to say, mom and dad were *not* stoked. But I was determined to proceed.

Prior to this moment, I had always been a shy, quiet, introverted, artistic child. I had never shown any previous interest in machinery, physics, or any other aspect of aerospace technology. But during a trip to NYC—a sightseeing tour in a chopper, soaring over the Statue of Liberty in Manhattan while the city twinkled below—I was enchanted.

"I want to learn how to fly. I want to become a pilot. This is what I want to do, *forever*," I decided, with all the arrogant, iron-clad conviction of a nineteen year old who had done basically nothing in life. "This is my calling."

As it turns out, I did *not* wind up pursuing a lifelong career in aviation.

I *did*, however, work my tail off to earn the money for pilot school, learn how to fly a Robinson R22 (two-bladed, single-engine light utility helicopter), complete a round trip solo flight from Long Beach Airport to Oxnard Airport, pass my check-ride exam, and successfully earn my private pilot's license.

On Christmas Eve, shortly after my twenty-first birthday, to celebrate earning my license, I flew around Long Beach Airport, making traffic patterns in the sky while my semi-stunned family watched from the ground below, probably thinking, *Well, dang. Who would have guessed? She actually did it.*

Even though I didn't go on to become a professional pilot (I ended up becoming a writer instead), learning to fly bolstered my self-esteem and confidence in a manner that forever altered the course of my life.

Once you accomplish something terrifying, alien, completely out of your comfort zone—something you're genuinely not sure you can do—with that type of victory under your belt, you are never the same.

After doing a nighttime flight over downtown Los Angeles, pretty much everything else in life felt like no sweat by comparison.

DURING HELICOPTER PILOT SCHOOL, I WAS FIRST INTRODUCED TO THE CONCEPT OF A PRE-FLIGHT CHECKLIST.

I was already pretty keen on lists. As a kid, I loved to write and I would often make lists of all kinds of things, such as my favorite types of unicorns (yes, there are many types) and business ideas (such as melting bars of soap in the microwave, adding bright food coloring, then shaping the old soap into new, horribly lumpy soap and selling it to neighbors—a business venture that did not work out).

But at pilot school, I was introduced to a very specific type of checklist, called a *Pre-Flight Checklist*.

As the name suggests, this is a checklist of things that you absolutely *must* do before departing for a flight. This is not a scrap of paper to be lightly perused and then ignored. Following this checklist means the difference between life and death.

I always followed my Pre-Flight Checklist with extreme attention to detail because, you know, I didn't want to fall careening from the sky to a fiery death.

The Pre-Flight Checklist is considered by most historians to be the "original" or "first" type of checklist. Like so many of humankind's greatest achievements, it was born out of necessity—and tragedy.

FROM A DEADLY CRASH, THE CHECKLIST WAS BORN.

It's October 30, 1935. Franklin D. Roosevelt is the current US President. If you're into astrology, the Sun is in Scorpio. Movies about cattle thieves, horses, and sheriffs are really having a moment.

On this day, at a field near Dayton, Ohio, Boeing Aircraft is planning a very special presentation for the US Military. It's the grand unveiling and debut flight of the Model 299, also known as the Boeing B-17 Flying Fortress.

The Model 299 was, at this point in history, the most advanced plane that the world had ever seen. It was as if everyone had been using rotary phones, and now, here came the iPhone. A marvel of technology. Boeing was hoping to dazzle the US Army Air Corps with this exquisite new plane, thereby securing a lucrative military contract.

Things do not go as planned.

Tragically, the plane lifts off, climbs for a few seconds, then nose-dives into the ground—killing two people. Three others were rescued from the wreckage. A horrific tragedy for the families of those who were lost, not to mention, a huge embarrassment for Boeing.

What went wrong? Was it a mechanical malfunction? No. Inexperienced pilots? No. After a thorough investigation, the sad truth came forth. The fatal crash happened all because the flight crew failed to do one crucial step: release the flight control gust locks. Why didn't they do this step? *They forgot.* Simple as that. They had too many steps to remember and they just forgot one.

After this catastrophe, Boeing vowed, "Never again." They developed a new system: the Pre-Flight Checklist. By completing this checklist, every vital step would be completed. Nothing would be skipped due to negligence, distraction, tiredness, forgetfulness, or any other human frailty.

Essentially, Boeing's leaders realized, "The human brain can only hold so much information/tasks/steps at a time. Even the most seasoned pilots are bound to forget things occasionally. By providing a list of things to check off, we can dramatically improve flight safety."

It worked.

In fact, this new system worked so well that many organizations followed Boeing's lead and brought checklists into their operations, too.

HOW DO YOU GET TO THE MOON, MAKE TOUGH BUSINESS DECISIONS, AND SAVE MILLIONS OF LIVES? MAKE A CHECKLIST.

NASA created a Launch Operations Checklist for the Apollo 11 moon voyage of 1969. This list was incredibly detailed (well over one hundred pages long) with every single step that needed to be taken to carry the astronauts to the moon and back. This checklist was so crucial to the mission's success that it was called "the fourth crew member."

Restaurateur Danny Meyer, founder of legendary restaurants like Gramercy Tavern, Union Square Cafe, and the international Shake Shack franchise, created a simple four-point checklist to help himself make smarter business decisions. As his restaurant empire continued to boom and expand, Meyer's personal checklist helped him to reduce what he called "progress anxiety." Thanks to his handy list, he could evaluate business opportunities using a short, consistent list of criteria, weed out the wrong opportunities, and focus on the right ones.

In 2008, the World Health Organization published a Surgical Safety Checklist. This nineteen-point list reduced the number of deaths due to infections and other preventable complications by 38 percent. Atul Gawande, a physician, public health researcher, checklist aficionado, and author of *The Checklist Manifesto*, calls this Surgical Safety Checklist an "absurdly simple" tool.

It's true. Checklists are often "absurdly simple."

So simple, in fact, that we sometimes think, *This whole process is unnecessary. I don't need to make a list. I'll just remember everything by myself.* But the "oh, I'll just remember it" strategy rarely works out!

In a world full of distractions, noise, and chaos, an absurdly simple tool is exactly what our beleaguered brains need. A checklist is like a form of mental medicine—the prescription for a weary, overstuffed mind.

LONG BEFORE AIRPLANES AND MOON LANDINGS: THE EARLY ORIGIN OF THE CHECKMARK SYMBOL.

While most historians credit Boeing with inventing the modern checklist—as we know and use it today—the checkmark symbol ✓ actually has much earlier roots.

During the Roman Empire, the letter "V" was used as shorthand for the word *Veritas*, meaning "truth". It's believed that during Roman times, putting a "V" next to something indicated "It's truly done" or "Yes, it's the complete truth."

Over the centuries—perhaps due to the fact that most people are right-handed and tend to write the letter "V" going from left to right—the tail on the right side of the "V" became elongated, leading to the checkmark symbol as we commonly see it today.

Veritas is not just a Roman word, but also a Roman Goddess—the Goddess of Truth. She's often depicted wearing white and holding a mirror. She's an elusive goddess, often hiding at the bottom of a sacred well. Perhaps the message we're meant to receive is that finding the truth is not always easy, and sometimes requires great effort to uncover.

I like the idea that whenever I check something off a list, it's like a quiet little moment of connection with the Goddess of Truth. Because there is no such thing as a "halfway" or "semi" checkmark. It's either a full, solid checkmark—or it's not done yet. There's no in between. With each checkmark, it's like saying, "*Veritas*, see? It's done. Really and truly done. It's the truth." I feel like this particular Goddess gets a thrill of delight every time an item is checked off.

Now that we've taken a historical tour through the world of checklists—from ancient goddesses to ambitious aviators—let's shift our focus to your individual life. In the next chapter, we'll look at some neuroscience: your brain on checklists.

CHAPTER THREE

The Science of Checklists

WHAT HAPPENS INSIDE YOUR BRAIN AND

BODY—ON A PHYSIOLOGICAL LEVEL—WHEN YOU

COMPLETE A CHECKLIST. WHY IT FEELS SO

INCREDIBLY SATISFYING TO MAKE A LIST AND

CHECK THINGS OFF.

YOUR BRAIN ON CHECKLISTS.

Most people agree that making a list and checking things off just intuitively feels "really good." But why is this? What's happening in your brain and body—on a physiological level—when you use a checklist?

There are many theories on why human beings love lists. Here, I've summarized a few leading theories—plus a few of my own personal ones.

CHECKLISTS ARE LIKE AN EXTRA STORAGE TANK FOR YOUR OVERWHELMED BRAIN.

Daniel Levitin, a neuroscience professor at McGill University, says that "most people can only hold about four things in their mind at a time."

Not 6,344 things. Just four.

Making a checklist is like creating an extra storage tank for your brain. You're helping yourself to remember all the extra things that your regular human brain can't successfully remember on its own.

This creates a feeling of emotional relief ("Ahhh, it's all down on paper, I know I'm not forgetting anything important"). Much like closing all the tabs on your internet browser, you're closing all the extra tabs in your brain. Subtracting and simplifying. This action feels soothing, which can help reduce the levels of *cortisol* (a hormone associated with panic, threat, and stress) throughout your body. When your cortisol levels drop, this leads to a relaxed and creative mind, deeper sleep, optimal digestion and metabolism, a stronger immune system, and overall, a life that just feels significantly *better*.

CHECKLISTS REDUCE DECISION FATIGUE.

Researchers from top universities like Stanford and Princeton have found that the more decisions you have to make every day, the more mentally exhausted you feel—a state known as *decision fatigue.*

When your brain is fatigued from excessive decision-making, this creates a feeling of overwhelm and fogginess (think: wandering aimlessly through the aisles of Target, feeling delirious because there are 9,046 different types of shampoo and you can't decide which one to buy). Decision fatigue also makes you more vulnerable to external influences like billboards, TV commercials, and peer pressure. Your willpower crashes to the ground. With a fatigued mind, swinging through the fast-food drive-through on your way home from work suddenly seems like a great idea while hitting the gym does not.

By creating a checklist, you're reducing your options from "unlimited" to "the items right here on this list," thereby reducing the number of decisions you need to make. For many people, this creates an immediate feeling of relief—and can help you avoid the dreaded state of decision fatigue.

CHECKLISTS FEEL REWARDING. (AND OUR BRAINS LOVE REWARDS.)

To quote the National Institute on Drug Abuse website, "the neurotransmitter *dopamine* teaches you to repeat pleasurable, rewarding activities."

In other words, if something feels good, you don't want to do it just once. You want to do it again, and again, and again.

For instance, you swipe on a dating app and get a flirty message from someone attractive. Ooh! It's fun to receive the attention. Dopamine tells you, "That felt good. Do it again." So you do.

Fast-forward several hours later. It's 3 a.m. You ought to be asleep because you need to wake up early for work tomorrow. Your fingers are practically falling off from excessive swiping—but you don't want to stop. You feel compelled to keep swiping because your brain's reward center is lit up like a Christmas tree. That's dopamine in full effect.

You can get that sweet dopamine rush from things like alcohol, drugs, accumulating "hearts" and "likes" on your social media posts, swiping, and texting. However, you can *also* get dopamine from experiences that are more nourishing—things that provide wonderful health benefits without a throbbing hangover the next morning. Things like hugging your child, gazing at the starry night sky, writing a love letter, stretching or working out, listening to your favorite music, lighting a fragrant candle, decluttering your desk so it's tidy and attractive, and of course, the simple satisfaction of checking an item off a checklist. All of these experiences can feel really rewarding, too.

YOU CAN GET "HOOKED" ON THINGS THAT ARE ACTUALLY GOOD FOR YOU. CHECKLISTS CAN HELP.

As Lauren Marchese writes in her article, "How Checklists Train Your Brain to be More Productive and Goal-Oriented," "when we feel the effects of dopamine, we're eager to repeat the actions that resulted in that success in the first place."

For instance, you promise yourself you'll drink a big glass of water first thing in the morning. You put "drink a big glass of water" on your checklist. You wake up. You drink the water. You check it off. You see that checkmark and feel a tiny moment of victory. "I did it!" This lights up the reward center of your brain—hello, dopamine! Dopamine says, "That felt good. Do it again." You feel compelled to keep going.

You want to complete the next item on your checklist, and the next, and the next—repeat, repeat, repeat—so you keep earning those delightful checkmarks and keep getting the dopamine-burst that you crave.

So instead of mindless internet scrolling (or another less-than-ideal habit), you're completing positive, productive, nourishing checklist items that are really good for you.

• • •

From the Ten Commandments in the Bible to Dua Lipa's catchy list of breakup tips in her pop song "New Rules" ("One: Don't pick up the phone, You know he's only callin' 'cause he's drunk and alone...") there's no doubt that human beings instinctively love lists.

We love making them. We love reading them. We love completing them. For all kinds of reasons, lists just "work" for our brains.

Later in this book, I'll share my personal checklist methods, including how to create a Daily Checklist, Loose-End Checklist, Seasonal Checklist, and other types of checklists.

But before we discuss how to make a checklist, first, there's a big question to consider...

HOW DO YOU WANT TO SPEND YOUR TIME?

What are your top priorities in life? What type of person do you aspire to be? Is there a philosophy, belief system, faith, or some other "approach to life" that makes sense to you?

Would you like to discover one?

This is what we'll discuss next.

By exploring these big questions, this is how you elevate your Daily Checklist from "just a bunch of stuff I need to do" to "a meaningful list that reflects what a 'good life' means to me."

CHAPTER FOUR

The Big Question: How Do You Want to Spend Your Time?

THE AVERAGE HUMAN LIFESPAN IS 37,580,400

MINUTES LONG. HOW DO YOU WANT TO SPEND

YOUR REMAINING LIFE-MINUTES? THIS IS A BIG

QUESTION. ONCE YOU'VE ANSWERED THIS BIG

QUESTION, THEN MOST OF LIFE'S SMALLER

QUESTIONS—LIKE WHICH ITEMS TO PUT ON

YOUR DAILY CHECKLIST—BEGIN TO FEEL CLEARER

AND SIMPLER.

The average human lifespan is 71.5 years, or 37,580,400 minutes.

How should you spend these precious life-minutes? What's the ideal use of your time?

There's no one correct answer to these questions. There are billions of possible answers, just like there are billions of people on planet earth.

The key, I feel, is to choose an answer that makes sense to *you*. You might call this answer a mission, purpose, belief system, organizing principle, faith, attitude, philosophy, or simply, *an approach to life*.

When you find an approach to life that makes sense to you, this creates a beautiful feeling of clarity.

Instead of feeling adrift in a sea of unlimited possibilities, you feel focused.

Instead of staring at a blank sheet of paper and wondering, *What should I do with my life? What are my priorities? What should I put on my checklist for tomorrow?* you feel clear about your next steps.

What is *your* approach to life?

If you're not sure, this section of the book will help.

CHOOSING YOUR PERSONAL APPROACH TO LIFE.

Different people have different ways of approaching this thing we call "life."

For my mom, life is all about pleasure, beauty, and love. The whole point of life, according to momma, is to laugh, kiss, eat dark chocolate, play the ukulele, make art, swim in the sea, smell the roses, and have fun with the people she adores most. Pleasure, beauty, and love are my mom's highest priorities—priorities which drive her decisions every day. This is her approach to life.

Your approach might be similar. Or your approach might be very different.

Below, you'll find a list of several different approaches for you to consider. Read the list. You might agree with some of these approaches—and disagree with others. Some of these approaches might immediately leap out at you—lighting up your body, making your heart beat a little faster, making you sit up a little taller, giving you an instinctive feeling of right-ness: "Yes! This makes sense to me! This is how I want to approach my life, organize my days, and spend my time!"

For instance, perhaps, as you read along, you notice that you really like the idea of approaching your life according to the Japanese principle of *kaizen*. Or maybe *kaizen* doesn't jive with you, but you're drawn to Todd Henry's concept of *dying empty*. Or maybe neither of those strike your fancy, but you're intrigued by how Dr. Sasha Heinz talks about *values*.

Pay attention to which approaches light you up.

This may clarify what's most important to you and how you wish to approach your life.

VALUES

Many psychologists—including my friend Dr. Sasha Heinz—recommend living according to your values.

Don't know what your values are? Dr. Heinz suggests you ask yourself questions like this: "What type of person do I aspire to be?" "What character traits do I admire most in others?" "How do I want to be remembered by my loved ones when I'm gone?"

Come up with a few words that sum up the type of person you aspire to be. For instance: *brave, conscientious, kind*. These are your top values.

Then, try to fill your daily life with activities that allow you to be this type of person. When an item on your checklist aligns with the values in your heart, this creates a feeling of wellbeing. Your brain goes, "Ahhhh. Yes. This feels right."

DOES THIS APPROACH RESONATE WITH YOU?
DO YOU LIKE THE IDEA OF DESIGNING YOUR LIFE
ACCORDING TO YOUR VALUES?

_____
_____
_____
_____
_____
_____
_____

WHAT KIND OF PERSON DO YOU ASPIRE TO BE?

_____
_____
_____
_____
_____
_____
_____

DESIRES

Danielle LaPorte, author of *The Desire Map*, suggests that you design your life based on one question: "How do you want to feel?"

How do you want to feel as you go about your typical daily life? Perhaps, for example, you want to feel: *relaxed, focused, affluent, generous,* and *creative.*

Okay. Well then, LaPorte says, fill your day with experiences that help you feel exactly that way. She calls this process *desire mapping.* Map out your day according to your desired feelings.

This allows for a great deal of flexibility, because there are infinite things you can do to generate the feelings you want. For instance, if you want to feel *generous,* you could donate $15 dollars to a charity, pay your niece's cellphone bill, give a $5 tip to your barista, or help out a friend with his job application. Any of those things (and countless other things) might allow you to feel generous. There are many ways to create the feelings you want.

DOES THIS APPROACH RESONATE WITH YOU?
DO YOU LIKE THE IDEA OF DESIGNING YOUR LIFE
ACCORDING TO YOUR DESIRES/FEELINGS YOU
WANT TO EXPERIENCE?

_____

_____

_____

_____

_____

_____

_____

ON A TYPICAL DAY OF YOUR LIFE, HOW WOULD YOU
LIKE TO FEEL?

_____

_____

_____

_____

_____

_____

_____

_____

KAIZEN

Kaizen is a Japanese word that means "improvement." This is
a popular concept in many business circles—the idea that a
company, team, or individual person can continually strive to
improve every day.

Always finding areas to refine. Always making progress. Always
learning. Always growing. Never reaching perfection—which
doesn't exist—but continually improving.

A kaizen attitude towards life would be: "Today is another chance
to improve. I can always do a little bit better than yesterday."

DOES THIS APPROACH RESONATE WITH YOU? DO
YOU LIKE THE IDEA OF DESIGNING YOUR LIFE
ACCORDING TO KAIZEN PHILOSOPHY?

_____

_____

_____

_____

_____

_____

_____

WHICH SKILLS (OR AREAS OF YOUR LIFE) WOULD
YOU ESPECIALLY LIKE TO IMPROVE?

_____

_____

_____

_____

_____

_____

SOHWAKHAENG

Sohwakhaeng is a Korean term that means "small but certain
happiness." Think: a warm cup of tea. Your favorite peanut butter
cookie. A single peony flower in a vase on your desk. The feeling
of clean sheets when you slip into bed. A hug from a dear friend.

Tiny moments that always make you feel good. That's the essence of sohwakhaeng.

A sohwakhaeng attitude towards life would be: "Life is all about feeling good. Experiencing joy, beauty, pleasure—that's the point. I always make sure to incorporate sohwakhaeng moments into each day."

DOES THIS APPROACH RESONATE WITH YOU?
DO YOU LIKE THE IDEA OF MAKING SOHWAKHAENG
A CENTRAL FOCUS FOR YOUR LIFE?

_____
_____
_____
_____
_____
_____
_____

WHAT ARE SOME OF YOUR FAVORITE
SOHWAKHAENG MOMENTS?

_____
_____
_____
_____
_____
_____
_____

SEXUAL ENERGY

Kim Anami is a sex educator who has studied the ancient philosophies of Daoism and Tantra for decades. Anami believes that your sex life should be your highest priority. Sex with a loving partner (or masturbation, if you're single) should be at the top of your daily to-do list, not the bottom.

Why? As she explains it, when your sexual energy is withering, then your entire life withers along with it. No sex life? Marriages crumble. Creativity dries up. Tense, brittle parents scream at their kids. Then the kids act out. There's a weary, dusty quality about you (tumbleweeds blowing across your ghost-town genitals) that others can sense. Flourishing sex life? Everything changes. You glow from the inside out. Everything in life feels imbued with new possibility.

Anami asserts that 99 percent of our problems could be cleared up if we start having what she calls *gourmet sex*—high quality, deep, meaningful, intimate, conscious sex. Lots of it.

DOES THIS APPROACH RESONATE WITH YOU? DO YOU LIKE THE IDEA OF MAKING SEX/INTIMACY A CENTRAL FOCUS FOR YOUR LIFE?

_____

_____

_____

_____

_____

_____

_____

IMAGINE YOU'VE REDESIGNED YOUR LIFE ACCORDING TO KIM ANAMI'S PHILOSOPHY. SEX IS NOW YOUR HIGHEST PRIORITY. THE #1 MOST IMPORTANT ITEM ON YOUR LIST. HOW MIGHT THIS CHANGE YOUR LIFE?

_____

_____

_____

_____

_____

_____

_____

DYING EMPTY

In his book, *Die Empty*, author Todd Henry points out that most people have a lot of wonderful dreams—projects they'd love to complete, trips they'd love to take, books they'd love to write, adventures they'd love to have, businesses they've love to launch.

But for various reasons—lack of resources, lack of confidence, inertia, laziness, fear of failure—most people never do the wondrous things they dream about. "Most people die," Henry says, "with their best work still inside of them."

Henry urges us to stop waiting and act now. Get everything out while you can, while there's still time. Don't die full, with all of your greatest dreams and best work still inside of you, unrealized. Die empty.

Henry is cautious to remind readers that when he says "die empty," this doesn't mean you should abandon your family, stop paying taxes, and disappear into the woods to hunt for a new species of rare pheasant, never to be seen again. Dying empty doesn't mean "abandoning all of your current responsibilities." Dying empty means that a portion of your life (four hours a week, ten minutes a day, whatever you can do) should be reserved for your greatest work.

DOES THIS APPROACH RESONATE WITH YOU? DO YOU LIKE THE IDEA OF APPROACHING EACH DAY OF YOUR LIFE WITH A "DIE EMPTY" ATTITUDE?

_____

_____

_____

_____

_____

_____

_____

WHAT IS A DREAM, GOAL, OR PROJECT YOU'VE ALWAYS LONGED TO DO—BUT HAVEN'T DONE YET?

_____

_____

_____

_____

_____

_____

_____

FAITH

Perhaps you're affiliated with a particular religion or spiritual practice. What does your religious/spiritual tradition say about what it means to lead a "good life"?

For instance, Jesus Christ urges us to be compassionate and generous to all beings, particularly those who are less fortunate.

If faith is important in your life, then you might want to plan your day in accordance with "what Jesus would do" "what Krishna would do" "what Allah would do" or whatever God(s) you follow.

IS FAITH IMPORTANT IN YOUR LIFE?

_____

_____

_____

_____

_____

_____

_____

WHEN IT COMES TO LEADING A "GOOD LIFE," WHAT
DO YOUR SPIRITUAL/RELIGIOUS TEXTS ADVISE
YOU TO DO? DO YOU AGREE WITH SOME OF THE
TEACHINGS YOU'VE RECEIVED, BUT NOT ALL?
WHICH RESONATE MOST STRONGLY WITH YOU?

_____

_____

_____

_____

_____

_____

NECESSITY

There are times in life when necessity rules the day. For instance,
your federal tax return is due tomorrow. If you don't file and make
your payment on time, there will be unpleasant consequences.
What are you to focus on today? Duh. Your tax return. That's the
top priority.

You might have a pressing matter that's business-related, financial,
or perhaps a health situation.

A few years ago, I had a bouldering (indoor rock climbing)
accident, fell to the ground, and broke my leg. I was rushed to
the emergency room, and soon after, got surgery and had a
metal plate installed on my fibula. For the next twelve weeks or so,
my #1 priority was resting, healing, doing physical therapy, and
learning how to walk again. Other things (emails, phone calls,
client meetings, etc.) were still part of my life, but these matters got

placed onto the back burner. Fixing my busted leg was my focal point—the most urgent necessity.

For those twelve weeks, this gave my life a refreshing feeling of simplicity and focus. I was in a great deal of physical pain, and hobbling around on crutches wasn't much fun. But at the same time, the beauty of the experience was that I had no confusion about how I ought to be spending my time.

IS THERE AN URGENT NECESSITY IN YOUR LIFE THAT NEEDS TO BE ATTENDED TO RIGHT AWAY, BEFORE ANYTHING ELSE? A FIRE THAT NEEDS TO BE PUT OUT? AN URGENT MATTER THAT DESERVES YOUR FULL AND UNDIVIDED ATTENTION?

_____

_____

_____

_____

_____

_____

_____

YOUR FINAL TWENTY-FOUR HOURS

If you had twenty-four hours left to live, what would you do with your time? (This is my favorite question.)

Would you have wild, primal sex with your partner? Watch the sunrise and sunset one last time? Cut a ripe mango into chunks, sit outside in the fresh air, hold your children close and inhale the sweet scent of their hair? Would you forgive everyone who ever wronged you? Make a fire-pit in the backyard, pull a blanket around you, and watch the crackling flames? Write a "thank you" letter to your greatest mentor?

Make a list of what you'd do if you had twenty-four hours left to live. If you start crying while you're writing your list, good. You're on the right track. This exercise can rapidly clarify what really matters to you, and what you value most in life.

A few years ago, I asked people to post their list online using the #MyFinal24 hashtag. Hundreds of people shared their lists, and each one is profoundly moving. If you're curious to see other people's lists, go to Instagram and search for #MyFinal24. You'll find a collection of lists posted by people of all ages, from all around the world.

I wrote a book, *So This Is the End: A Love Story,* inspired by this question. The book follows the fictional character of Nora Hamilton as she navigates her final twenty-four hours on earth. Shortly after the book's release, I had a conversation with a woman who'd read the story. I loved this woman's perspective on the twenty-four hour question. To paraphrase, here's what she told me:

> "Alex, I've been thinking about this whole idea of living like you have just one day left. I love this idea so much, but I feel stuck. Because I kept thinking, 'Well I can't take a hot air balloon ride every day! I can't throw a huge party with a live band every day! I can't eat an entire chocolate cake every day! I have a job. I have bills. I have responsibilities. And realistically, I need to plan for the future.' Then it occurred to me, it's not really about the hot air balloon ride. It's more about the simple things. I can kiss my husband every day. I can watch the sunset every day. These small things are possible even on the busiest of days— and these small things are the moments that make life feel so rich and meaningful."

DOES THIS APPROACH RESONATE WITH YOU? DO
YOU LIKE THE IDEA OF APPROACHING YOUR LIFE
WITH A "THIS MIGHT BE MY FINAL DAY" ATTITUDE?

_____
_____
_____
_____
_____
_____
_____
_____

IF YOU HAD TWENTY-FOUR HOURS LEFT TO LIVE,
WHAT WOULD YOU DO WITH YOUR TIME?

_____
_____
_____
_____
_____
_____
_____
_____

RECAP

What's your approach to life?

What matters to you most of all?

How do you want to spend your time each day?

These are some of the big questions we've been exploring for the last several pages.

To recap, here are some different ways to approach your life and make decisions about how to spend your time. You could:

- Find your top *values* and then plan your day based on these values.

- Decide how you want to feel, your *desires*, and then plan your day to generate these feelings.

- Adopt a *kaizen* attitude towards life and view every day as a chance to improve, filling your day with activities that allow you to grow and refine different areas of your life.

- Adopt a *sohwakhaeng* attitude towards life and fill your day with moments of "small but certain happiness."

- Make *sexual energy* your #1 priority and design your whole day around this.

- Focus on *dying empty*, making sure you're emptying the tank a little bit more each day.

- Let your religious/spiritual *faith* guide you into making decisions around how to spend your time.

- Plan your life based on sheer *necessity*. What absolutely needs to be done first?

- Make a list of what you'd do in your *final twenty-four hours* of life. Live this way—or as close as possible—every day.

Maybe one of those approaches resonates with you strongly. Maybe several do. Maybe you could combine two of them together (for instance: values + dying empty or kaizen + faith) to create an approach to life that feels right for you.

Again, there's no one correct way to journey along through this thing we call life.

You get to choose the approach that feels best to *you*.

TRUST YOUR HUT.

I believe we all have an inner voice, which I call your "hut" (heart + gut) that is always speaking to us.

When I feel rushed, pressured, stressed, and frenzied, all of this anxiety drowns out the sound of my hut and I can't hear my hut clearly. It's like trying to hear a teeny-tiny cricket in a crowded, noisy bar. It doesn't work. I can't hear.

But then, when I relax and become quiet, that's when I hear my hut speak the loudest.

With all of these big questions—what's my approach to life? how should I spend my time?—what is your hut's opinion? What does your hut have to say? Trust your hut.

Let your hut fill in the blanks:

"MORE THAN ANYTHING ELSE, _____
ARE THE THINGS THAT REALLY MATTER TO ME."

_____

_____

_____

_____

_____

_____

_____

_____

"AT THE END OF MY LIFE, WHEN I'M DYING, AS LONG
AS I KNOW THAT I'VE _____
THEN I CAN DIE IN PEACE."

_____

_____

_____

_____

_____

_____

_____

_____

"AT THE END OF MY LIFE, WHEN I'M DYING, AS LONG
AS I KNOW THAT I'VE _____
THEN I CAN DIE IN PEACE."

_____

_____

_____

_____

_____

_____

_____

_____

"THERE ARE MILLIONS OF DIFFERENT THINGS I COULD DO WITH MY TIME. MILLIONS OF DIFFERENT WAYS I COULD LIVE MY LIFE. BUT FOR ME, PERSONALLY, AN IDEAL DAY WOULD LOOK LIKE _____, AND AN IDEAL LIFE WOULD INCLUDE _____. THAT'S THE KIND OF LIFE I WANT."

_____

_____

_____

_____

_____

_____

_____

_____

"MY APPROACH TO LIFE IS _____ _____."

_____

_____

_____

_____

_____

_____

_____

_____

_____

Your hut is very wise—and never leads you astray.

• • •

HURTLING THROUGH TIME AND SPACE.

By now, I hope you're feeling clear about your approach to life—and how you want to spend your remaining time on this planet. Feel totally clear? Amazing! Still don't feel totally clear? Well, me neither, and guess what? Most people don't!

Everyone is mostly just guessing and grasping wildly in the dark. I think it's perfectly normal to swing from clarity to uncertainty and then back to clarity again.

To quote one of my favorite TV characters of all time:

"WE ARE BUT VISITORS ON THIS ROCK,
HURTLING THROUGH TIME AND SPACE AT
66,000 MILES AN HOUR. TETHERED TO A
BURNING SPHERE BY AN INVISIBLE FORCE
IN AN UNFATHOMABLE UNIVERSE."
—SPECIAL AGENT FOX MULDER,
THE X-FILES

Ultimately, everything is a gigantic mystery. We're riding an earth-ship through the cosmos and nobody really knows why we're here, what happens after we die, or how we ought to approach life and spend our time. Many people wonder. Many people guess. But nobody knows absolutely "for sure."

So if everything is a mystery, then what's the point of making a checklist to plan your day? Why bother writing down your goals for the next season or year? What's the point of any of this?

I asked my friend Gemma Stone, a brilliant psychologist who, incidentally, looks exactly like Ariel from *The Little Mermaid*, for her thoughts. I love her perspective.

Gemma told me:

"It's true, we're hurtling through time and space. And it's true, ultimately, nobody knows why we're here. Nobody hands you a piece of paper and says, 'Here, read this. This is the reason why you exist.' Since nobody hands you a 'reason', then you get to choose the reason for yourself. You get to decide."

We leaned against my kitchen counter, drinking coffee while she continued.

"By making a checklist for your day," Gemma said. "That's like taking the 'reason' you've chosen and putting it into words, putting things into a plan. You're taking the mystery and making meaning out of it."

"Right," I agreed. "And I've noticed, for me, having a checklist helps me feel so much calmer."

Gemma laughed and said, "Yes! When you have a checklist for your day, it's like a seatbelt on a rocket ship. You're still hurtling through time and space. Everything is still crazy and mysterious. But you feel a little calmer, a little more secure. Your nervous system settles down. You can relax a bit. You can actually *enjoy* the rocket ride—instead of feeling terrified and overwhelmed and spinning into an existential crisis every single day of your life."

I like Gemma's seatbelt metaphor a lot—and I feel the same way. For me, making a checklist does indeed feel like a seatbelt—providing just enough security, steadiness, and comfort to help me exhale and enjoy the wild ride of life.

Life is full of mystery.

Making a checklist brings a little calm, focus, and meaning into the madness.

WHAT

LIGHTS

YOU

UP?

CHAPTER FIVE

The Daily Checklist

HOW TO CREATE A DAILY CHECKLIST THAT

INCLUDES TASKS YOU NEED TO COMPLETE, AS

WELL AS MOMENTS YOU WANT TO EXPERIENCE.

THINGS YOU NEED TO DO AND THINGS YOU

WANT TO DO. BRIEF. ONE PAGE. REFRESHINGLY

SIMPLE. ACHIEVABLE. REALISTIC. CUSTOMIZED

JUST FOR YOU.

MAKING A DAILY CHECKLIST CAN CHANGE YOUR LIFE.

In this chapter, I'll teach you my method for creating a Daily Checklist.

As the name suggests, a Daily Checklist is a checklist for *one day* of your life, not your entire year, season, or month. Just one day.

PURPOSE OF THE DAILY CHECKLIST.

The purpose of the Daily Checklist is to help you:

- Feel calm, focused, and organized as you move through your day.
- Make a plan for your day that reflects your personal approach to life, a plan that feels meaningful to you.
- End each day feeling proud of yourself—with a visual record of all the things you've accomplished. (All of those victorious checkmarks!)

I want to emphasize that a Daily Checklist is not just "a list of stuff to do." It's more than that. Your Daily Checklist includes *tasks* you need to complete and *moments* you want to experience. Things you *need* to do and things you *want* to do. Both.

In the previous chapter of this book, we explored questions like, "What is your approach to life?" "What really matters to you?" "How do you want to spend your time on the planet?" Your Daily Checklist is an opportunity to take your answers to those questions and translate them into specific items that you can check off throughout your day. You're taking big ideas and making them small and achievable.

If an archaeologist five hundred years from now discovered one of your Daily Checklists—say, buried in a time capsule—this archaeologist would learn a lot about you just by glancing at it. They'd learn what you care about, what your top priorities are, and what a "good life" looks and feels like to you.

ONE DAY. ONE PAGE.

Ideally, your Daily Checklist is short enough to fill just one sheet of standard 8.5" x 11" paper. One day. One page. Not multiple pages.

Brevity is key. You want your Daily Checklist to include the most important tasks and moments of your day (which feels good), but without being excessively detailed and lengthy (which feels overwhelming).

Too many pages...is not good. I've tried this. Personally, it doesn't work well for my brain. I've found that having a multi-page checklist for my day usually leaves me feeling exhausted/anxious/overwhelmed before the day has even begun! One page feels much more doable.

"NIGHT BEFORE" PLANNING IS IMPORTANT.

You will make your checklist for tomorrow...*today*.

For instance, if today is December 9, then today you'll make a Daily Checklist for December 10.

That way, when you wake up tomorrow on December 10, your checklist for the day is already ready, prepared, waiting for you. Your day can begin on a clear, focused note ("Okay, it's a brand new day, here we go! I know what I'm doing today!") instead of confusion/overwhelm/inertia/etc.

This becomes a beautiful daily ritual. Towards the end of each day—perhaps in the late afternoon, early evening, or as you're winding down for bedtime—take a few moments to consider,

"What's my plan for tomorrow?" Then take a few minutes to update your Daily Checklist so it's ready for tomorrow. Get your checklist sorted out before you head off to bed. Then you can sleep deeply, knowing you're not forgetting anything important. Your plan for tomorrow is already prepared and waiting for you!

AN EVOLVING LIST.

No two days in life are exactly the same.

One day, you might be moving into a new apartment. Another day, you're resting at home recuperating from knee surgery. Another day, you're grieving a significant loss in your life and your mind is distracted and foggy. Another day, you're driving across the state to attend a family reunion and you'll be in the car for six hours rather than working at your desk. Your resources (time, energy, money, mental/physical health) and circumstances might vary from day to day and from season to season.

For this reason, your Daily Checklist is an evolving document. You update it daily, setting your intentions and making your plan for the next day. Your plan for tomorrow might be very similar (practically identical) to the one today, or it might not be!

You can always make your Daily Checklist longer/shorter/ more demanding/less demanding/different depending on what's happening in your life right now and the resources you have available.

CHECKMARK, NOT STRIKE-THROUGH.

This is a small but important detail. As you complete items on your Daily Checklist (or any checklist), please mark these with a checkmark. *Don't* draw a line through completed items and strike

them out. Why? Because it's important to see—and celebrate—
your victories throughout the day rather than obliterating them!

I once chatted with a woman who kept her Daily Checklist on the
Notes app on her phone (which I don't recommend—for reasons I'll
explain later—real paper is way better than a digital screen). As she
completed items from her checklist, she would delete these items
from her app.

At the end of each day, when she glanced at her phone, what
did she see? A list of everything she *hadn't* done yet. Meanwhile,
everything she *had* done—all of her accomplishments—gone.
Deleted. Invisible.

You can imagine the impact this had on her mental state! She
would usually end the day feeling anxious and self-critical ("Ugh, I
didn't get enough done!") rather than ending the day on a positive
note ("Awesome, look at everything I completed!").

So, I strongly encourage you to mark completed items with a
victorious checkmark, or with an X, star, heart, smiley face, lightning
bolt, or some other symbol that indicates "Success!" to you, rather
than striking out, covering up, or deleting items you've completed.

OVERALL FLOW, BUT NOT RIGID.

Your Daily Checklist shows the overall flow of your day, from the
moment you wake up to your final moments of the night. However,
it doesn't need to be rigid, tight, and restrictive. This is about setting
a clear intention for your day, but it's not about "perfection."

For instance, you *don't* necessarily need to complete your Daily
Checklist "perfectly" in order from start to finish, top to bottom.
You can do this if you want. You can also keep things flexible and
skip around. As long as everything (or at least most things) get
completed by the end of the day, great! Sometimes the order
matters. Sometimes it doesn't.

Also, you *don't* need to put exact times for everything you plan to do—like this: 6 a.m. Drink smoothie, 6:15 a.m. Iron shirt and pants, 6:35 a.m. Call a Lyft for the airport, and so forth. You can put exact times if you want—some people like doing this and find it helpful— but personally, I find that approach a little too rigid. I like to give myself more freedom.

When I look at my Daily Checklist, I say to myself, "This is my overall plan for the day. This is what I intend to do and experience tomorrow. But not necessarily in this exact order. Nothing is rigid."

DAILY CHECKLIST TEMPLATE.

Here is a template for creating a Daily Checklist.

You can also download this template in several formats (Word doc, Pages doc, and PDF) at: alexandrafranzen.com/checklists

Tasks and moments can be put into any order you want, for instance: Task - Moment - Task - Moment, or Task - Task - Moment - Moment, or whatever makes sense for your day.

This template is intended to get you started, but please know that you can modify it however you want. You can add items, subtract items, re-arrange certain items—whatever feels instinctively right to you.

Next, I'll walk you through the step-by-step instructions.

CHECKLIST FOR [DATE]

[Word, phrase, quote,
or message that inspires you.]

- FIRST MOMENT:
- EASY WIN:
- EASY WIN:
- EASY WIN:
- TASK:
- TASK:
- TASK:
- MOMENT:
- MOMENT:
- MOMENT:
- UNEXPECTED/SPONTANEOUS/EXTRA CREDIT:

- UNEXPECTED/SPONTANEOUS/EXTRA CREDIT:

- UNEXPECTED/SPONTANEOUS/EXTRA CREDIT:

- FINAL MOMENT:

HOW

TO MAKE

A DAILY

CHECKLIST

STEP-BY-STEP INSTRUCTIONS: HOW TO MAKE A DAILY CHECKLIST.

These instructions are being imparted to you...in the form of a checklist! Whoa! A checklist about how to make a checklist! Is your mind blown? You can check steps off as you go along, which feels so satisfying.

● GATHER YOUR SUPPLIES.

If you're writing your checklist by hand, you will need:

- A few sheets of blank paper—lined paper, graph paper, whatever you prefer.
- Something to write with—a pen, pencil, marker, whatever you want to use.

If you're typing your checklist (as I usually do) you will need:

- Something to type with, like a tablet or computer.
- A blank document to type into—or download and use the template I've provided to you.
- A printer.
- Ink cartridges for your printer.
- Blank paper for your printer.

You will also need:

- Somewhere to display your finished checklist, like a bulletin board, clipboard, or folder.

(To see all my favorite paper/office products, and my favorite inexpensive printer, look at the Recommended Books, Websites & Other Resources section of this book.)

● SET THE SCENE.

Before making your checklist, set yourself up for success. This looks different for everyone, but for you, this might mean:

- Making sure you have a quiet, peaceful space to work.
- Turning your phone to vibrate—or better yet, silent or completely off.
- Making sure your kids are supervised, your schedule is clear, and you won't be interrupted.
- Playing inspiring music.
- Lighting a candle.
- Putting a plant or pot of flowers by your workspace, just because it makes you feel good.
- Setting aside some water, coffee, tea, or snacks.
- Whatever else you need to do to set yourself up for success.

● GET A BLANK SHEET OF PAPER—OR IF YOU'RE TYPING, OPEN A DOCUMENT. AT THE VERY TOP, PUT "CHECKLIST FOR" AND THEN TOMORROW'S DATE.

For example:

CHECKLIST FOR
THURSDAY, DECEMBER 10

ADD A MESSAGE THAT'S MEANINGFUL TO YOU.

Right after the date, add an inspiring word, phrase, quote, mantra, song lyric—some type of message that's meaningful to you. Perhaps a short message of inspiration, motivation, or encouragement, like a pep talk from a friend. Something to pull your mindset into a positive place.

Some of my favorite phrases include:

- Keep breathing.
- Keep going. One tiny goal at a time.
- Not today, Satan!
- Stay focused. You can do this.
- The best is yet to come.
- Things are moving in the right direction.
- Today is a brand new day.
- Today is not over yet.
- Today is going to be a great day.
- You are powerful and capable.
- You can do challenging things.
- You're doing a great job.
- You're stronger than you think.

CHECKLIST FOR
THURSDAY, DECEMBER 10

Keep going. One tiny goal at a time.

● ADD YOUR VERY FIRST MOMENT.

Think about the very first moment you'd like to experience tomorrow.

Right after you wake up, what's a brief moment that would get your day started on a positive note?

For instance, would you like to begin your day with:

- A moment of prayer.
- A moment of meditation.
- A moment of gratitude.
- Thirty seconds of stretching.
- Three deep breaths.
- Ten push-ups or jumping jacks.
- Kissing your spouse/partner.
- Cuddling your kids.
- Something else?

Choose your first moment of the day. Put this as your very first checklist item.

CHECKLIST FOR
THURSDAY, DECEMBER 10

Keep going. One tiny goal at a time.

- TAKE THREE DEEP BREATHS, OPEN THE CURTAINS, AND ADMIRE THE DAWN SKY.

● ADD A FEW EASY WINS.

Below your first moment of the day, put a few tiny goals that you feel very confident you can complete. These are very small promises that you're 99.9 percent certain you can keep—without much effort or strain. Think: easy wins.

Examples of tiny goals/easy wins might be:

- Drink a big glass of water.
- Drink some delicious coffee.
- Make your bed.
- Put lotion on your elbows.
- Text Diana to say, "I miss you and I love you."
- Wash your face.
- Set a timer for five minutes and write a journal entry.

By adding a few easy wins to your checklist, this helps you begin your day on a victorious note. As you check off these first few tiny goals, you feel rewarded—thanks to dopamine in your system. You want to keep going. You feel proud of yourself. There's a feeling of action, aliveness, movement, momentum—things are in motion! Your day has barely begun, and it's already off to a great start!

CHECKLIST FOR
THURSDAY, DECEMBER 10

Keep going. One tiny goal at a time.

- TAKE THREE DEEP BREATHS, OPEN THE CURTAINS, AND ADMIRE THE DAWN SKY.
- DRINK A BIG GLASS OF WATER.
- MAKE YOUR BED.
- HAVE A CUP OF COFFEE AND SOME DARK CHOCOLATE-COVERED ALMONDS.
- SIT BY THE WINDOW AND READ A FEW PAGES OF **DIE EMPTY.**

ADD A FEW TASKS.

What are some tasks you need to complete tomorrow? Add a few of these to your checklist.

When I say "task," this means: "an important responsibility, commitment, or urgent/time-sensitive necessity."

Examples of tasks might be:

- Meet with Rachel to discuss the marketing proposal.
- Call repair company to discuss the pipe that keeps leaking.
- Email Laurence and Shonda to figure out a meeting date/time that works for everyone.
- Set a timer for 30 minutes and make flashcards to study for Spanish exam.
- Set a timer for 60 minutes and work on grant application.
- Set a timer for 60 minutes and answer as many emails as possible.
- Drop rent check into the mail before 5 p.m.

You might think, "But I have one hundred little tasks I need to complete tomorrow! Do I need to put every single task on my checklist? That would make an extremely long list!"

Firstly, maybe one hundred tasks is too many tasks for one day. Are you being somewhat unrealistic, or holding yourself to an unreasonably high standard? Many people wildly overestimate what is possible/reasonable to complete in a single day. We over-cram our schedules and set ourselves up for disappointment. Remember that you're planning one *day* of your life, not one *month*.

Secondly, no, you don't need to put every single little thing you intend to do. Just put the main tasks that feel the most important/crucial/significant to you. Things you *definitely* want to accomplish. Think: the main colors of the painting. The main notes of the song. The main milestones of your day. The feeling is: "If I handle these tasks, and nothing else, I will feel quite proud of myself."

CHECKLIST FOR
THURSDAY, DECEMBER 10

Keep going. One tiny goal at a time.

- TAKE THREE DEEP BREATHS, OPEN THE CURTAINS, AND ADMIRE THE DAWN SKY.
- DRINK A BIG GLASS OF WATER.
- MAKE YOUR BED.
- HAVE A CUP OF COFFEE AND SOME DARK CHOCOLATE-COVERED ALMONDS.
- SIT BY THE WINDOW AND READ A FEW PAGES OF **DIE EMPTY**.
- DROP THE KIDDOS OFF AT SCHOOL.
- SET A TIMER FOR 60 MINUTES AND ANSWER AS MANY EMAILS AS POSSIBLE.
- MEET WITH MEGAN TO DISCUSS THE EVENT BUDGET AND STAFFING QUESTIONS.
- SET A TIMER FOR 60 MINUTES AND WRITE A ROUGH DRAFT OF THE JANUARY E-NEWSLETTER.
- SEND E-NEWSLETTER TO JORDAN FOR EDITING/PROOFREADING.

ADD A FEW MOMENTS.

What are some moments you want to experience tomorrow? Add a few of these to your checklist.

When I say "moment," this means: "an experience that feels pleasurable, delightful, enjoyable, beautiful, meaningful" or that makes you feel "thriving, flourishing, happy, healthy" or just "more alive."

Examples of moments might be:

- Write a tiny "I love you" note and hide it inside Sonia's school lunchbox.
- Call mom and tell her that hilarious dolphin story.
- Eat lunch outside in the sunshine, not inside at your desk.
- Watch a *Saturday Night Live* comedy sketch on YouTube.
- Listen to a two-minute guided relaxation meditation.
- Take the 6 p.m. spin class.
- Stretch for five minutes by candlelight before bedtime.

CHECKLIST FOR
THURSDAY, DECEMBER 10

Keep going. One tiny goal at a time.

- TAKE THREE DEEP BREATHS, OPEN THE CURTAINS, AND ADMIRE THE DAWN SKY.
- DRINK A BIG GLASS OF WATER.
- MAKE YOUR BED.
- HAVE A CUP OF COFFEE AND SOME DARK CHOCOLATE-COVERED ALMONDS.
- SIT BY THE WINDOW AND READ A FEW PAGES OF **DIE EMPTY**.
- DROP THE KIDDOS OFF AT SCHOOL.
- SET A TIMER FOR 60 MINUTES AND ANSWER AS MANY EMAILS AS POSSIBLE.
- MEET WITH MEGAN TO DISCUSS THE EVENT BUDGET AND STAFFING QUESTIONS.
- SET A TIMER FOR 60 MINUTES AND WRITE A ROUGH DRAFT OF THE JANUARY E-NEWSLETTER.
- SEND E-NEWSLETTER TO JORDAN FOR EDITING/PROOFREADING.
- TAKE A WALK FOR THIRTY MINUTES AND LISTEN TO THE NEW EPISODE OF **SO OBSESSED**.
- TEXT ELLEN BECAUSE HER HIP SURGERY HAPPENED A FEW DAYS AGO. SEND A HUG. SEE HOW SHE'S DOING.
- LIE ON THE FLOOR FOR ONE FULL MINUTE, CLOSE YOUR EYES, AND JUST BREATHE.
- HAVE A GLASS OF MALBEC WHILE LISTENING TO LEONARD COHEN'S LATEST ALBUM.
- DURING DINNER, ASK THE KIDDOS, "WHAT WAS THE BEST PART OF YOUR DAY?" AND SHARE STORIES.

ADD A FEW BLANK LINES.

Inevitably, unexpected things arise in life.

You're rolling along through your day and then:

- The check engine light pops on inside your car. Yikes. You need to get that checked out.

- You suddenly remember it's Kate's birthday and you meant to send her a gift.

- You spontaneously decide to meet up with friends for happy-hour cocktails at the pier.

- You're really "in the zone" with a work project. A very productive groove. You decide to keep going and complete a few additional pieces of the project that you hadn't planned to do—like extra credit.

Somewhere on your checklist, add a few blank lines for these unexpected/spontaneous/extra credit items—which might arise tomorrow, or might not! Who knows?

CHECKLIST FOR
THURSDAY, DECEMBER 10

Keep going. One tiny goal at a time.

- TAKE THREE DEEP BREATHS, OPEN THE CURTAINS, AND ADMIRE THE DAWN SKY.
- DRINK A BIG GLASS OF WATER.
- MAKE YOUR BED.
- HAVE A CUP OF COFFEE AND SOME DARK CHOCOLATE-COVERED ALMONDS.
- SIT BY THE WINDOW AND READ A FEW PAGES OF **DIE EMPTY**.
- DROP THE KIDDOS OFF AT SCHOOL.
- SET A TIMER FOR 60 MINUTES AND ANSWER AS MANY EMAILS AS POSSIBLE.
- MEET WITH MEGAN TO DISCUSS THE EVENT BUDGET AND STAFFING QUESTIONS.
- SET A TIMER FOR 60 MINUTES AND WRITE A ROUGH DRAFT OF THE JANUARY E-NEWSLETTER.
- SEND E-NEWSLETTER TO JORDAN FOR EDITING/PROOFREADING.
- TAKE A WALK FOR THIRTY MINUTES AND LISTEN TO THE NEW EPISODE OF **SO OBSESSED**.
- TEXT ELLEN BECAUSE HER HIP SURGERY HAPPENED A FEW DAYS AGO. SEND A HUG. SEE HOW SHE'S DOING.
- LIE ON THE FLOOR FOR ONE FULL MINUTE, CLOSE YOUR EYES, AND JUST BREATHE.
- HAVE A GLASS OF MALBEC WHILE LISTENING TO LEONARD COHEN'S LATEST ALBUM.
- DURING DINNER, ASK THE KIDDOS, "WHAT WAS THE BEST PART OF YOUR DAY?" AND SHARE STORIES.

ADD YOUR FINAL MOMENT.

Think about the very last moment you'd like to experience tomorrow, shortly before you head off to bed.

What's a final moment that would allow your day to feel "complete"? Something that would allow you to fall asleep feeling content, satisfied, and proud of yourself?

Perhaps you'd like to conclude your day with:

- A few minutes of reading.
- A few minutes of journaling.
- A nice shower or bath.
- One more kiss from your sweetheart.
- Pre-loading your coffee maker so it's ready for you tomorrow morning.
- Reading a bedtime story to your kids.
- A moment of gratitude for the roof over your head.
- Something else?

Choose your final moment of the day. Put this as your last checklist item.

CHECKLIST FOR
THURSDAY, DECEMBER 10

Keep going. One tiny goal at a time.

- TAKE THREE DEEP BREATHS, OPEN THE CURTAINS, AND ADMIRE THE DAWN SKY.
- DRINK A BIG GLASS OF WATER.
- MAKE YOUR BED.
- HAVE A CUP OF COFFEE AND SOME DARK CHOCOLATE-COVERED ALMONDS.
- SIT BY THE WINDOW AND READ A FEW PAGES OF **DIE EMPTY**.
- DROP THE KIDDOS OFF AT SCHOOL.
- SET A TIMER FOR 60 MINUTES AND ANSWER AS MANY EMAILS AS POSSIBLE.
- MEET WITH MEGAN TO DISCUSS THE EVENT BUDGET AND STAFFING QUESTIONS.
- SET A TIMER FOR 60 MINUTES AND WRITE A ROUGH DRAFT OF THE JANUARY E-NEWSLETTER.
- SEND E-NEWSLETTER TO JORDAN FOR EDITING/PROOFREADING.
- TAKE A WALK FOR THIRTY MINUTES AND LISTEN TO THE NEW EPISODE OF **SO OBSESSED**.
- TEXT ELLEN BECAUSE HER HIP SURGERY HAPPENED A FEW DAYS AGO. SEND A HUG. SEE HOW SHE'S DOING.
- LIE ON THE FLOOR FOR ONE FULL MINUTE, CLOSE YOUR EYES, AND JUST BREATHE.
- HAVE A GLASS OF MALBEC WHILE LISTENING TO LEONARD COHEN'S LATEST ALBUM.
- DURING DINNER, ASK THE KIDDOS, "WHAT WAS THE BEST PART OF YOUR DAY?" AND SHARE STORIES.
- _____
- _____
- _____
- RIGHT BEFORE BED, TAKE A RELAXING SHOWER AND THEN SLIP INTO BED, ALL NICE AND CLEAN. SWEET DREAMS!

● READ THROUGH YOUR CHECKLIST. MAKE REVISIONS IF NEEDED.

Read your checklist from top to bottom.

As you read, notice if you sense uneasy feelings—like dread, anxiety, heaviness, or overwhelm.

If you feel uneasy, that's a sign that your checklist is "not quite right." Maybe it's too long, too complicated, too daunting. Maybe you're trying to cram an excessive number of items into one day. Or maybe you've got that nagging sense that you're forgetting something important.

Take a few moments to notice how you're feeling. Then revise your checklist accordingly.

Is there anything you could remove from your list and save for another day? Is there anything you could delegate? Anything you could cancel? Is there any way you could make your day a little easier for yourself? Make some adjustments.

● DECIDE: "IS IT DONE?"

How do you know when your checklist is done?

You know it's done when you feel a sense of "right-ness."

For you, this sense of right-ness might feel like relief, contentment, calm, or an instinctive feeling in your hut (heart + gut) that tells you, "Okay, this is done."

It's that moment when you look at your checklist and you think something like:

- "Yes, this looks like a really good day."
- "I feel energized looking at this list, not exhausted."
- "This feels reasonable. I can do this."

- "I'm looking forward to all (or at least, most) of this."
- "This is going to feel great."
- "This is the kind of life I want to lead."
- "This feels like a healthy balance of tasks and moments."
- "I'll feel really content/satisfied/proud at the end of this day."

All done? Feeling good? Feeling right? Then your checklist is complete! Congratulations!

PUT YOUR CHECKLIST WHERE YOU'LL SEE IT—FIRST THING IN THE MORNING.

If you wrote your checklist by hand, then you're all set.

If you typed it, then print it out. Ideally, your Daily Checklist will fit on one page.

Put your checklist where you'll see it—first thing in the morning. For instance, pin it to a bulletin board that's right smack in the center of your bedroom. Or put it on a clipboard and put that clipboard right by your coffee maker, or right by your bed.

Let this checklist be one of the very first things you see and hold when you begin your day tomorrow.

And then tomorrow, focus on your list, and check things off throughout the day.

At the end of the day, celebrate all of your beautiful checkmarks! Great job! Look at all those tasks you completed! Look at all those beautiful moments you experienced! So wonderful!

There might be some things you didn't check off. Perhaps you ran out of time, didn't have enough energy, got distracted, got scared, got stuck, or got derailed by some other obstacle. That's okay. Put this un-checked item onto your checklist for the next day. Try again.

Try to focus more on celebrating the things you *did*, rather than harshly criticizing yourself for the things you didn't.

KEEP GOING. REPEAT DAILY.

Creating your first Daily Checklist might take a bit of time, but this process gets faster the longer you do it.

If you're using a computer, you can save a Daily Checklist document on your desktop. Use this doc to speed things along. Once a day, open the doc. Keep certain items the same—for instance, perhaps your first moment of the day, final moment of the day, and first couple of easy wins will be the same, day after day. Change a few items for tomorrow. Print it out. Boom. You're all done.

It takes time for new habits to settle into place. Give this some time. See how it feels to create a Daily Checklist for ten, fifteen, or twenty days in a row. Is this new habit making your life easier? Calmer? Happier? Do you feel more focused? Do you feel prouder of yourself at the end of each day? What changes do you notice?

PS: If you're proud and excited about your Daily Checklist and want to show it off, you can:

- Post a photo of your checklist on social media and tag with #TheChecklistBook
- Text a photo of your checklist to someone you love ("Look what I made!").
- Email a photo of your checklist to me: hello@alexandrafranzen.com. (I love seeing people's checklists! It fills me with ecstatic delight.)

SAMPLE DAILY CHECKLISTS.

Here are a few more Daily Checklists—filled out—to give you more examples of what these can look like.

CHECKLIST FOR THURSDAY, DECEMBER 10

> You are building
> the future you want, today.

- WAKE UP AND SPEND THREE MINUTES IN SEATED MEDITATION.
- DO TEN PUSH-UPS TO WAKE UP YOUR BODY AND BRAIN.
- MAKE YOUR BED.
- FILL UP YOUR WATER BOTTLE.
- WALK TO THE CAFETERIA AND GET A HEALTHY BREAKFAST.
- WALK ACROSS THE QUAD TO THE LIBRARY.
- SET A TIMER FOR 30 MINUTES AND MAKE ANATOMY FLASHCARDS.
- SET A TIMER FOR 30 MINUTES AND PRACTICE/MEMORIZE/USE ANATOMY FLASHCARDS.
- BREAK! TAKE A 10 MINUTE WALK OUTSIDE IN THE FRESH AIR.
- EMAIL PROFESSOR RUDD TO CONFIRM MEETING TIME (TOMORROW?) TO DISCUSS ESSAY.
- SEND A TEXT TO MOM AND DAD, SAYING, "THANK YOU FOR HELPING TO SEND ME TO COLLEGE. *I* LOVE YOU."
- SEND A TEXT TO VANESSA TO CONFIRM A MEET-UP TIME TO STUDY FOR KINESIOLOGY EXAM.
- SET A TIMER FOR 90 MINUTES AND FINISH WRITING FUNCTIONAL MEDICINE ESSAY.
- UPLOAD ESSAY TO GRAMMARLY TO CHECK FOR TYPOS, MISSING WORDS, ETC.
- CELEBRATE! YOU'RE DOING GREAT! TREAT YOURSELF TO A FANCY ICED COFFEE.
- IF YOU FEEL TIRED, GO FOR ANOTHER 10 MINUTE WALK AROUND CAMPUS.
- TAKE A MOMENT TO STARE UP AT THE SKY, WATCH THE CLOUDS FLOAT BY, NO ACTION, JUST BE.

RIGHT BEFORE BED, TAKE TWO MINUTES TO BREATHE DEEPLY. CLOSE YOUR EYES AND VISUALIZE PASSING YOUR EXAMS AND EARNING EXCELLENT SCORES. YOU CAN DO THIS.

CHECKLIST FOR THURSDAY, DECEMBER 10

Things are moving in the right direction.

- WAKE UP AND PLAY "YOU CAN'T STOP ME" BY ANDY MINEO. GET PUMPED! IT'S GOING TO BE A GREAT DAY!
- DO WIM HOF BREATHING EXERCISE.
- HAVE A CUP OF TEA AND READ **DIE EMPTY** BY TODD HENRY FOR A FEW MINUTES.
- SET A TIMER FOR 30 MINUTES. CHOOSE TOPICS FOR THE NEXT THREE EMAIL NEWSLETTERS.
- EMAIL DRAFT TO AARON AND ASK HIM TO DOUBLE-CHECK FOR TYPOS/ISSUES.
- EAT AN EPIC TOASTED BAGEL WITH AVOCADO, TOMATO, SRIRACHA, AND A FRIED EGG ON TOP.
- SET A TIMER FOR 30 MINUTES. FINISH DESIGNING "CUSTOMER APPRECIATION PARTY" INVITES.
- SET A TIMER FOR 60 MINUTES. PUT INVITES INTO ENVELOPES, PUT ADDRESSES, SEAL, AND STAMP.
- DROP INVITES INTO THE MAIL. ALL DONE! FINALLY! YES!
- STRETCH (ESPECIALLY CALVES/HAMSTRINGS) AFTER RUNNING.G
- TAKE A LONG SHOWER AND SHAVE.
- EMAIL JESS AND ASK FOR A SPECIAL FAVOR. "COULD YOU TEACH ME HOW TO WRITE A PRESS RELEASE, PLEASE?"
- FIND A CREATIVITY-BOOSTING GUIDED MEDITATION ON YOUTUBE.
- PLAY MEDITATION, CLOSE EYES, AND FOLLOW ALONG.
- SPEND 15 MINUTES BRAINSTORMING/WRITING DOWN A FEW MORE CREATIVE MARKETING IDEAS TO GENERATE SALES!
- LISTEN TO A COMEDY PODCAST **(YOU MADE IT WEIRD)** TO LAUGH AND WIND DOWN FOR THE DAY.
- SPOON WITH INARA, KISS DEEPLY, HOLD HER CLOSE.
-
-
- BEFORE BED, TAKE A FEW MOMENTS OF GRATITUDE FOR THE CLIENTS/CUSTOMERS WHO'VE SHOWN UP IN THE PAST. SEND A MENTAL "THANK YOU" TO EACH PERSON.

CHECKLIST FOR THURSDAY, DECEMBER 10

You have so many
valuable qualities and skills.

- DO A BIIIIIIIIG, LONG, FULL-BODY STRETCH IN BED. GOOD MORNING!
- PLAY CHILL MUSIC, LIKE "IN RAINBOWS" BY RADIOHEAD.
- SPLASH COOL WATER ON YOUR FACE.
- MORNING YOGA STRETCHES WITH THE KIDDOS.
- ASK KIDDOS, "WHAT'S YOUR WORD OF THE DAY?"
- PACK NOTEBOOK, PEN, LAPTOP, CHARGER, AND WATER BOTTLE.
- DROP THE KIDS OFF AT SCHOOL.
- HEAD TO SHARK'S COFFEE AND FIND A GOOD SPOT TO WORK.
- SET A TIMER FOR 30 MINUTES. MAKE A LIST OF CRITERIA/QUALITIES THAT YOUR "IDEAL JOB" WOULD HAVE. WHAT MATTERS MOST TO YOU?
- TAKE A MENTAL BREAK. LISTEN TO INSPIRING MUSIC, TAKE A WALK, GET SOME FRESH AIR, RESET YOUR MIND.
- EMAIL THE CAREER COACH THAT SARAH RECOMMENDED TO INQUIRE ABOUT FEES/RATES.
- TEXT MOLLY TO CONFIRM THAT SHE'S DOING AFTERNOON CARPOOL PICK-UP TODAY.
- GRAB GROCERIES FOR DINNER TONIGHT: VEGGIE TACOS.
- HEAD HOME, BLAST MUSIC, HAVE A SWEEPING/VACUUMING PARTY AND TRY TO MAKE IT FEEL FUN! (HA!)
- WATCH **HOW TO FIND THE WORK YOU LOVE** TED TALK BY SCOTT DINSMORE.
- DURING DINNER, ASK THE KIDDOS, "WHAT WAS THE BEST PART OF YOUR DAY?" AND SHARE STORIES.
-
-
-
- TAKE A LONG, HOT SHOWER. (TAKE A MOMENT OF GRATITUDE FOR CLEAN, RUNNING WATER.)
- MAKE SURE YOU DON'T HAVE PHONE/IPAD/TECH IN THE BEDROOM. MAKE IT A CALM ZONE.
- TRUST THAT YOU ARE CAPABLE, RESOURCEFUL, AND SMART, AND THINGS ARE GOING TO WORK OUT.

NOTES

NOTES

CHECKLIST FOR

CHECKLIST FOR

CHECKLIST FOR

CHECKLIST FOR

CHAPTER SIX

The Loose-End Checklist, Seasonal Checklist, Survival Checklist, and More

CREATING A DAILY CHECKLIST CAN CHANGE YOUR

LIFE. BEYOND THE DAILY CHECKLIST, THERE ARE

MANY OTHER CHECKLISTS YOU CAN CREATE.

LEARN HOW TO CREATE A LOOSE-END CHECKLIST,

SEASONAL CHECKLIST, SURVIVAL CHECKLIST,

MARKETING CHECKLIST, AND CHECKLISTS FOR

SPECIAL OCCASIONS, LIKE YOUR BIRTHDAY.

THE LOOSE-END CHECKLIST.

Do you have a million random things swirling around in your mind—
personal stuff, professional stuff, all kinds of loose ends that you
want to tie up?

Try making a Loose-End Checklist.

You can do this once a year, once a month, or whenever you have
that icky, anxious feeling that makes your head spin.

I feel waves of sweet relief whenever I make a Loose-End Checklist.
It feels so good to get all of these bits and bobs out of my head
and down on paper. When I do this, my brain immediately feels
much quieter. And *completing* the Loose-End Checklist feels even
better! Each checkmark drawn feels like putting a gold coin into my
self-esteem bank. It feels amazing to handle these matters instead
of ignoring them.

Here is a template for creating a Loose-End Checklist.

You can also download this template in several formats (Word doc,
Pages doc, and PDF) at: alexandrafranzen.com/checklists.

This template is intended to get you started. Modify it however
you want. Add categories, subtract categories, add more items—
whatever feels instinctively right to you.

 LOOSE-END CHECKLIST

Goal: Tie up all of the following
loose-ends by [date].

FINANCES

[Example: Find out why I keep getting
that weird $5 checking account fee
every month.]

- _____
- _____
- _____

HEALTH

[Example: Schedule annual physical exam
with Dr. Park.]

- _____
- _____
- _____

FRIENDS AND FAMILY

[Example: Send a 'thank you' card to
Sarah for the awesome birthday gift.]

- _____
- _____
- _____

EMAIL/SOCIAL MEDIA/DIGITAL LIFE

[Example: Go through inbox and
unsubscribe from all those newsletters I
don't want anymore.]

- _____
- _____
- _____

WORK

[Example: Total up hours for the Clear
project and send an invoice.]

- _____
- _____
- _____

HOME

[Example: Fix the squeaky
closet door.]

- _____
- _____
- _____

MISCELLANOUS THINGS

[Example: Return boots that don't fit and
get correct size or store credit.]

- _____
- _____
- _____

THE SEASONAL CHECKLIST.

Every summer, my friend Susan Hyatt creates her Summer Bucket List—a list of all of the beautiful things she wants to experience over the summer. Susan's list includes things like, "Jump topless into the lake!" "Eat a buttermilk biscuit sandwich with fried chicken and honey." "Sunbathe in a pineapple-print bikini."

I loved this idea so much—and I've started doing it, too.

It's really fun to make a checklist of meaningful experiences that you want to have this spring, summer, winter, or fall. These experiences can be big, small, public, private, close to home, far away, expensive, free—anything you can dream up.

When I'm making a Seasonal Checklist, I like to make mine really *big*. Get a large piece of butcher paper, poster paper, or other surface that takes up a good deal of space. Write things out in huge letters with a thick marker pen. Check things off all season long! At the end of the season, you can take a photo of your completed list as a memento of everything you've experienced.

Here is a template for creating a Seasonal Checklist. You can use this same template to create an Annual Checklist (whole year, not just one season) too.

You can also download this template in several formats (Word doc, Pages doc, and PDF) at: alexandrafranzen.com/checklists.

This template is intended to get you started. Modify it however you want. Add categories, subtract categories, add more items— whatever feels instinctively right to you.

SPRING/SUMMER/FALL/WINTER
❧❧ CHECKLIST ❧❧

EXPERIENCES—ALONE
[Example: Drive to the beach and meditate by the water at dawn.]

- _____
- _____
- _____

EXPERIENCES—WITH PEOPLE I LOVE
[Example: Take a Soca dance class with Kate.]

- _____
- _____
- _____

MUSIC
[Example: Make an epic summer playlist with my favorite songs.]

- _____
- _____
- _____

FOOD
[Example: Eat a perfectly crisp, cool, sweet slice of watermelon.]

- _____
- _____
- _____

NATURE
[Example: Have a picnic in the park, enjoying the sky and trees... with no cellphone.]

- _____
- _____
- _____

BIG/WILD/CRAZY
[Example: Book a last-minute, totally spontaneous flight to Vegas!]

- _____
- _____
- _____

THE SURVIVAL CHECKLIST.

Sometimes, you just don't want a big, thrilling, *everything-I-long-to-do-this-summer* checklist. Sometimes, you're not focused on exciting adventures—you're just trying to *survive*.

I was in a long-term relationship with a man for five years—traveling the world, having countless adventures, opening a business, raising a puppy—deeply in love, best friends as well as lovers. It was the most powerful romantic relationship of my entire life. And then it ended.

This breakup was startling, disruptive, and completely rocked my self-esteem. Without over-sharing too much, the circumstances of our breakup left me wondering things like, "Am I not sexy enough for him? Not interesting enough? Not lovable enough? Why aren't I enough?" Painful questions engulfed me.

I found myself struggling to sleep, losing my appetite, and sobbing constantly. I couldn't think clearly. Sometimes it felt like I couldn't even breathe. Ordinary daily tasks—like answering emails—felt completely overwhelming. During this time, a close friend commented that I looked like a "zombie." That's exactly how I felt. Dead inside.

Our breakup was lengthy and complicated, taking many months to unfold because we owned a home together and our lives were very enmeshed. To help myself navigate this emotionally challenging time, I made a special checklist for myself, which I called my *Survival Checklist*.

A Survival Checklist is a very short list of things you can do to navigate a hard time—be it a breakup, divorce, death, stressful career transition, physical or mental illness, or anything else that feels really tough.

Your Survival Checklist includes steps you can take to feel a tiny bit better, calmer, stronger, more empowered, and more grounded during this time.

Here is a template for creating a Survival Checklist.

You can also download this template in several formats (Word doc, Pages doc, and PDF) at: alexandrafranzen.com/checklists.

This template is intended to get you started. Modify it however you want. Add categories, subtract categories, add more items—whatever feels instinctively right to you.

SURVIVAL CHECKLIST

BASIC HYGIENE

[Example: Brush your teeth.]

- _____
- _____
- _____
- _____
- _____
- _____

SUPPORT—FRIENDS AND FAMILY

[Example: Text your friend Melissa if you feel scared and need to talk.]

- _____
- _____
- _____
- _____
- _____
- _____

SUPPORT—PROFESSIONAL

[Example: Ask Liz for the name/email of the divorce attorney that she hired.]

- _____
- _____
- _____
- _____
- _____
- _____

MENTAL HEALTH/PHYSICAL HEALTH/SELF-CARE

[Example: Take three deep breaths to settle your nervous system.]

- _____
- _____
- _____
- _____
- _____
- _____

THE MARKETING CHECKLIST.

Do you run a business or side-business, work as a freelancer or consultant? If you're self-employed, marketing is probably a central part of your life. Many people loathe marketing and view it as a tedious, stressful chore. Countless colleagues have said to me, "I love my work—*except* for the marketing part."

I used to dislike marketing, too—until I had a realization that completely changed my attitude about it. One day, it occurred to me that *marketing can feel like an art project.*

For instance:

- Writing an inspiring email newsletter is an *art project*—and it's marketing.

- Launching a podcast to expand your audience is an *art project*—and it's marketing.

- Planning a beautiful customer appreciation party is an *art project*—and it's marketing.

- Designing an awesome flyer to promote your new program is an *art project*—and it's marketing.

- Making cute "come in for a free coffee" gift cards to build awareness about your new restaurant is an *art project*—and it's marketing.

Once I had this realization (marketing = making art), suddenly I felt excited about marketing! Instead of thinking, *I love making art—but I hate marketing*, I began to think, *I love making art—and marketing can feel like a creative art project!*

While driving to my favorite coffee place one morning, I saw a person dressed in a T-Rex dinosaur costume, dancing on the street corner and waving a sign that said "Car Wash". I had to blink—is this really happening? Whaaaaat? It was the most hilarious thing I'd seen all week. You better believe I pulled into the lot to get my car washed—immediately! I didn't even *need* a car wash, but suddenly, I desperately *wanted* one! Haha! I also made a video of the dancing dinosaur and texted that video to five different friends, saying, "Y'all need to get down here a.s.a.p. and see this amazing dinosaur and get your car washed!" This company's marketing approach totally worked on me!

This is a perfect example of what I mean when I say that marketing can feel like a creative art project. Marketing doesn't have to be dull and soul-sucking. It can be artistic. It can be meaningful. It can be beautiful. It can also be silly, delightful, enchanting, and highly entertaining. Like a dancing dinosaur.

Here is a template for creating a Marketing Checklist.

You can also download this template in several formats (Word doc, Pages doc, and PDF) at: alexandrafranzen.com/checklists.

Project: Briefly describe your project, service, program, product, book, class, event tickets—whatever you're selling.

Why: Write down three reasons why you want to sell this. Aside from "making money," which is definitely important, why else is this important to you?

Sales goal: Number of sales/enrollments/sign-ups/etc. that you want to reach.

Timeline: When will you start marketing, and for how many days/weeks/months?

Victory/Reward: How will you celebrate completing this Marketing Checklist? Come up with a few ways to reward yourself for your hard work.

This template is intended to get you started. Modify it however you want. Add categories, subtract categories, add more items—whatever feels instinctively right to you.

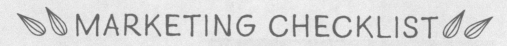 MARKETING CHECKLIST

PROJECT: _____

WHY: _____

SALES GOAL: _____

TIMELINE: _____

FRIENDS AND FAMILY

[Example: Email five of your closest friends, one by one, personally, and let them know about this new project!]

○ _____
○ _____
○ _____

FLYERS AND POSTERS

[Example: Design a fun flyer and pin up 20 around town.]

○ _____
○ _____
○ _____

SNAIL MAIL

[Example: Send handwritten "thank you" cards to the last five clients—and invite them to hire you again.]

○ _____
○ _____
○ _____

EMAIL NEWSLETTER

[Example: Write an email newsletter to shine a spotlight on recent clients and their victories.]

○ _____
○ _____
○ _____

MEDIA OUTREACH

[Example: Drop off a beautiful box of product samples and press releases at the local newspaper office.]

○ _____
○ _____
○ _____

PREVIOUS CUSTOMERS AND CLIENTS

[Example: Host a customer appreciation party and use this as a chance to debut a new product line too.]

○ _____
○ _____
○ _____

SOCIAL MEDIA

[Example: Do an Instagram story with a behind-the-scenes tour of the new studio under construction, and announce the grand opening date to get everyone super excited!]

○ _____
○ _____
○ _____

SUPER CREATIVE, WEIRD, WILD, AWESOME

[Example: Dress up like a dinosaur and dance on the street corner with a sign. LOL.]

○ _____
○ _____
○ _____

VICTORY/REWARD: [Example: Treat yourself to a hot lather and shave at the barbershop.]

○ _____   ○ _____
○ _____   ○ _____

THE WORKOUT CHECKLIST.

Once, I attended a group exercise class. In the middle of class—during a particularly challenging sequence when we were all huffing, puffing, sweating profusely, silently cursing and wishing we were literally anywhere but inside that room—the instructor reminded us, "It's a privilege to run. It's a privilege to move. It's a privilege to be here in this gym." I was so moved by these words. I'd never thought about fitness like that before. It was an attitude adjustment that I definitely needed, and one that I've never forgotten.

It's true. Exercise is a privilege. To have a human body. To have the ability to breathe, sweat, and move. *To be alive.* All of this is a privilege. Many people view exercise as a tedious chore—something to grimly suffer through. But it's not a chore. It's a privilege and a celebration of what your amazing body can do.

If you have a very busy schedule and a very limited amount of time to work out—say, thirty minutes, three times a week—that's okay. Whatever time you've got, get in there and make those minutes count! It's totally possible to have a fantastic workout even if you've only got thirty minutes to spare. Even ten minutes of movement is better than nothing and provides so many mental and physical health benefits.

Whether you're heading to work out at the local gym, park, community center, inside your living room or bedroom, in your garage, backyard, or anywhere else, make yourself a Workout Checklist to plan out your session from start to finish. That way, you can head into your workout feeling focused and organized—instead of wandering around aimlessly, wondering what to do, and dawdling by the elliptical machines. Advance planning makes such a big difference.

Nowadays, I carry a clipboard and pen with me whenever I go to the gym. I check things off my Workout Checklist as I'm going along. By the end of my workout session, I'm covered in sweat—and my list is covered in checkmarks! Victory!

I have a few different Workout Checklists that I keep on my computer (so I can update them periodically and re-print), including:

- A treadmill/weights workout that's mostly focused on lower body.

- A treadmill/weights workout that's mostly focused on upper body.

- A full-body workout that requires no gym equipment/can be done outdoors.

- The J-Lo workout, which one of Jennifer Lopez's trainers posted online. (Google it!)

- A relaxing bedtime yoga, foam roller, and stretching routine.

Here is a template for creating a Workout Checklist.

You can also download this template in several formats (Word doc, Pages doc, and PDF) at: alexandrafranzen.com/checklists.

Victory/Reward: Complete at least three workouts this week to unlock a special reward! Come up with a few ways to reward yourself for your hard work.

This template is intended to get you started. As always, please modify it however you want. Every body is unique. The workout that feels right for you might be very different from the workout that feels right for me. Use common sense when planning your workout. Be safe. Be kind to yourself. It's great to conquer new fitness goals, however, don't push yourself to the point of strain or injury. Always consult with a healthcare and/or fitness professional if you have exercise-related questions.

WORKOUT CHECKLIST

WARM UP
[Example: Slow walking lunges across the room, back and forth, for sixty seconds.]

- _____
- _____
- _____

CARDIO
[Example: Jog on the treadmill for five minutes at 3 percent incline.]

- _____
- _____
- _____

WEIGHTS
[Example: Lat pulldown machine. Twelve reps. Rest. Repeat three times.]

- _____
- _____
- _____

MUSIC
[Example: Make an epic summer playlist with my favorite songs.]

- _____
- _____
- _____

CORE
[Example: Hold forearm plank for at least ninety seconds.]

- _____
- _____
- _____

EXTRA CREDIT
[Example: Thirty mountain climbers!]

- _____
- _____
- _____

STRETCH/COOL DOWN
[Example: Wide leg stance, forward fold. Hold at least thirty seconds.]

- _____
- _____
- _____

VICTORY/REWARD
[Example: Treat myself to tickets for the new Keanu Reeves movie!]

- _____
- _____
- _____

A FEW OTHER CHECKLISTS YOU MIGHT LIKE TO CREATE

There are an infinite number of checklists you could create.

Here are some of my favorite checklists I've created over the last few years:

THE BIRTHDAY CHECKLIST

Make a checklist of magical moments you want to experience on your birthday.

For instance:

- Eat a slice of funfetti cake.
- Get a free birthday drink from Starbucks.
- FaceTime with mom and dad.
- Treat yourself to some fresh flowers.
- Make a beautiful wish for the upcoming year.

THE VACATION CHECKLIST

Make a checklist of experiences you want to have while you're visiting Tokyo, London, the island of Maui, Boise, Austin, or wherever you're going.

I did this on a recent trip to New York City. I kept my Vacation Checklist in my hotel room and checked things off as my trip flowed along. My NYC checklist included things like:

- Get an amazing cheeseburger at Cask Bar & Kitchen.
- Get nutritious vegan food at Dr. Smood.
- See a stand-up show at the Comedy Cellar.

- Take a Buti Yoga class at BMVNT.
- Go see *Hadestown* on Broadway on opening night.
- Go to a meditation class.
- Meet up with Ben and Iele for tea.
- See Ally and meet her new husband.
- Complete the Orange Theory triathlon.
- SoulCycle class with Robert.

And so forth.

I really enjoyed making a Vacation Checklist. It helped me avoid FOMO (Fear of Missing Out) and stay focused on the moments I really wanted to experience. This Vacation Checklist also became a cool record of my trip—like a journal entry full of memories.

If you're traveling with your family, or with other people, you can collaborate and build a Vacation Checklist together. Have everyone choose a few items to add to the list. Other/similar lists: Road Trip Checklist, Travel Checklist, Cruise Checklist, Family Reunion Checklist, etc.

THE STAYCATION CHECKLIST

Be a tourist in your own hometown. Make a checklist of experiences you want to have in your own city—for instance:

- Walk through that park you always drive by.
- Wander through the old, historic cemetery.
- Go to the public library and finally get a library card.
- Check out that museum you've been meaning to visit.
- Attend the free Tai Chi class that happens down the block.

It's incredible how many experiences are available to us—often, for free—right in our zip code, or even right in our own backyard.

THE SELF-ESTEEM CHECKLIST

Psychologist Guy Winch, PhD, author of *Emotional First Aid*, says that our emotional wellbeing requires daily maintenance. Just like you take care of your dental hygiene daily/consistently (brushing and flossing your teeth to prevent them from rotting out of your mouth), you have to take care of your emotional hygiene daily/consistently too.

What are some small things you could do to boost your self-esteem, confidence, and sense of wellbeing?

When I make a Self-Esteem Checklist, it usually includes things like:

- Text a compliment to a friend to make their day a little brighter.
- Do five push-ups just because you can. You're strong!
- Write down three things you're good at.
- Take a little extra time with your skin/hair. Get extra cute.
- Make a small promise to yourself and then keep it.
- Make a Self-Esteem Checklist and then check things off over the course of one day, one week, or one month—whatever timespan you want. Notice if your emotional state improves as a result of these steps you're taking.

It's amazing what a little bit of emotional hygiene can do.

THE _____ CHECKLIST

What other kinds of checklists could you make? The options are endless.

Maybe you want to make…

- A checklist for a specific project—recording a podcast, remodeling your kitchen, planning a party.

- A checklist for a big life change—like starting college, becoming a parent, or transitioning to a new profession.
- A checklist of beautiful date nights you want to experience with your partner.
- A checklist of non-TV-related activities to do with your family in the evenings.
- A checklist of 39 things you want to do before your 39th birthday, or 65 things to do before your 65th birthday, etc. (Special credit to my friend Sarah Von Bargen for this idea— so brilliant!)

What are some checklists you might like to create?

- _____
- _____
- _____
- _____
- _____
- _____
- _____
- _____
- _____

SHARE YOUR CHECKLISTS WITH ME, ANYTIME.

I love seeing people's checklists. Send me a photo of your latest checklist. Or send a quick email and tell me which is your favorite checklist idea and why: alexandrafranzen.com/contact.

NOTES

NOTES

GOAL: _____

- _____
- _____
- _____
- _____
- _____

- _____
- _____
- _____
- _____
- _____

- _____
- _____
- _____
- _____
- _____

- _____
- _____
- _____
- _____
- _____

- _____
- _____
- _____
- _____
- _____

- _____
- _____
- _____
- _____
- _____

- _____
- _____
- _____
- _____
- _____

- _____
- _____
- _____
- _____
- _____

GOAL: _____

GOAL: _____

GOAL: _____

VICTORY/REWARD

PROJECT: _____

WHY: _____

SALES GOAL: _____

TIMELINE: _____

○ _____
○ _____
○ _____
○ _____
○ _____

○ _____
○ _____
○ _____
○ _____
○ _____

○ _____
○ _____
○ _____
○ _____
○ _____

○ _____
○ _____
○ _____
○ _____
○ _____

○ _____
○ _____
○ _____
○ _____
○ _____

○ _____
○ _____
○ _____
○ _____
○ _____

○ _____
○ _____
○ _____
○ _____
○ _____

○ _____
○ _____
○ _____
○ _____
○ _____

VICTORY/REWARD:

○ _____ ○ _____
○ _____ ○ _____

PROJECT: _____

WHY: _____

SALES GOAL: _____

TIMELINE: _____

○ _____
○ _____
○ _____
○ _____
○ _____

○ _____
○ _____
○ _____
○ _____
○ _____

○ _____
○ _____
○ _____
○ _____
○ _____

○ _____
○ _____
○ _____
○ _____
○ _____

○ _____
○ _____
○ _____
○ _____
○ _____

○ _____
○ _____
○ _____
○ _____
○ _____

VICTORY/REWARD:

○ _____   ○ _____
○ _____   ○ _____

CHAPTER SEVEN

Checklist Troubleshooting

A FEW STRUGGLES THAT MIGHT ARISE—AND

GENTLE SUGGESTIONS FOR EACH ONE. FOR

INSTANCE, WHAT TO DO IF YOU MAKE A DAILY

CHECKLIST, BUT YOU NEVER COMPLETE

EVERYTHING AND THEN FEEL BAD ABOUT ALL THE

BOXES YOU DIDN'T CHECK OFF. OR, WHAT TO

DO IF YOU'RE SOMEONE WHO VALUES FREEDOM

AND SPONTANEITY, SO THE WHOLE IDEA OF

MAKING A CHECKLIST FEELS WAY TOO RIGID

FOR YOU. AND OTHER COMMON CHECKLIST-

RELATED DILEMMAS.

> "I MAKE MY DAILY CHECKLIST. BUT THEN I NEVER FINISH EVERYTHING ON MY LIST. AT THE END OF EACH DAY, I SEE ALL OF THOSE UN-CHECKED BOXES AND I FEEL BAD ABOUT MYSELF."

In this situation, you have three options:

- Change your *checklist*. (Make it shorter. Fewer items. Tinier goals. Be more realistic about what you can actually accomplish in a single day.)

- Change your *attitude*. (Decide it's okay if you don't finish everything. Be gentler with yourself. Give compassion to yourself. Find a way to feel at peace with whatever number of items you complete—whether it's one item on your checklist, half your checklist, or the full checklist.)

- Change *both*.

Personally, I recommend changing both. Changing your attitude is often the harder of the two.

To adjust your attitude, try telling yourself something like this:

- It's okay that I didn't finish everything on my list. I did my best. It's been a great day.

- I might not be completely "done," but progress has been made!

- Things are moving in the right direction.

- I will celebrate all of my victories rather than feeling bad about the boxes I haven't checked yet.

- Tomorrow is a new day. Another chance to complete things from my list.

- Feeling stressed and criticizing myself won't help me complete things any faster. It just makes me feel heavy and distressed and slows me down. So, I'm going to be kind to myself rather than critical.

- Not everything needs to be finished today, this week, or even this year. I don't need to rush. I can take my time.
- It's important to be compassionate with myself.
- I will speak to myself in a kind, encouraging tone of voice, just like I'd speak to a child or friend.
- Or another phrase that you like.

I've said this before, but it bears repeating: most people wildly overestimate what is possible/reasonable to complete in a single day! We often behave like we have 240 hours in a day rather than 24. We hold ourselves to an unreasonable standard of productivity—like we're robots rather than human beings who need to rest, sleep, bathe, relax, etc.

I definitely have this over-scheduling tendency, which is why I have to continually check in with myself and ask, "Is this realistic? Or is this an unreasonable plan?"

Overall, I feel it's much better to put *fewer* items on your checklist, and then feel pleasantly surprised by how much you completed, rather than putting tons and tonnnnnnns of items on your checklist, and then feeling miserable that you didn't finish everything.

"THERE'S ALWAYS THIS 'ONE THING' ON MY LIST THAT I DON'T DO. AND IT'S USUALLY SOMETHING IMPORTANT. WHY DO I KEEP AVOIDING THIS ONE THING?!"

Avoidance! It's so frustrating. There could be many reasons why you keep avoiding this "one thing."

When I'm avoiding something, it's usually because I feel a lot of heavy, complicated, negative emotions surrounding this particular checklist item—like guilt, shame, or fear.

If this is happening for you, I recommend enlisting some help.

Talk to a therapist, mentor, or coach.

Text a friend and ask them to give you a pep talk.

Even better, reach out to someone you love and ask them to be with you—face to face, heart to heart, in real life, right by your side—while you complete this difficult checklist item. If they can't be there physically, ask them to Skype or FaceTime with you and beam in virtually.

Your friend can sit with you and provide moral support while you send that difficult email, make an appointment with the divorce attorney, call the credit card debt management company, make cremation arrangements for your pet, or whatever emotionally challenging thing you need to do.

You can tell your friend, "Please be with me. Please help me to actually do this. I need some support/accountability/a hug/a friendly face/a hand to hold." Whatever you need, ask. Having someone there can make all the difference.

> "IS IT BETTER TO MAKE A SEASONAL CHECKLIST FIRST—AND THEN MAKE A DAILY CHECKLIST? THINK BIG, ZOOM OUT—THEN ZOOM IN? OR THE OTHER WAY AROUND? ZOOM IN—THEN ZOOM OUT?"

Either way can work!

You might want to think big—zoom out—and make a Seasonal Checklist or even an Annual Checklist. Write down your biggest priorities. Then based on your Seasonal Checklist or Annual Checklist, you design your Daily Checklist accordingly—choosing daily steps that move you closer and closer to those bigger priorities.

However, if you're feeling really overwhelmed right now—stressed about unpaid bills, struggling to focus on your work, drowning in too many priorities, depleted, bogged down by low energy levels—maybe this isn't the moment for big, visionary planning. Instead, focus on putting together your Daily Checklist for tomorrow. Not the whole season. Not the whole year. Just one day of your life.

What could you do tomorrow to steer your life in the direction you want? What could you do to feel a tiny bit better, calmer, steadier, and more proud of yourself? Put those steps on your Daily Checklist. Focus on those steps for now. Don't worry about what you need to accomplish next week or next month. Take things one day at a time. Later, when you're feeling a bit calmer and less overwhelmed, perhaps you'll feel ready to "go big" and write down bigger goals, dreams, moments, experiences, and so forth.

> **"I ALWAYS HAVE TOO MUCH TO DO. I'M NOT GOOD AT SAYING 'NO' TO PEOPLE, AND AS A RESULT, MY SCHEDULE IS ALWAYS CRAMMED WITH WAY TOO MUCH STUFF. HELP?!"**

My very wise therapist, Ryan Brown, once said to me: "We have unlimited love, but limited time."

So true. You might have an infinitely big heart and an unlimited desire to support and help others, but you still only have twenty-four hours per day. There are limits to your time and energy. Sometimes you have to say no.

A few years ago, I came up with an approach for saying no that really has helped me.

This approach can be summed up like this:

- "Congratulations on _____."
  (Offer some genuine praise/excitement/encouragement)

- "It sounds like you want _____."
  (Echo back the request they've made)

- "I won't be able do that, but here's what I can offer instead:
  _____."
  (Say no and then offer something helpful—for instance, something you're willing to do instead, or perhaps a resource, website, book, someone to hire, something else that might help)

Here's an example. Let's say a friend emails me and says:

> "Hey Alex! Could you read my book manuscript and give some feedback on my writing? I know you're busy, but it would mean so much to me."

I could reply by saying:

> "Congratulations on writing a book! That's a major accomplishment. I'm so proud of you.
>
> It sounds like you want some feedback on your book manuscript—and maybe some editing/proofreading help, too?
>
> My schedule is very full at the moment and I don't have space for new projects, so I won't be able to do this. I wish I could! Thanks for understanding.
>
> If you're looking for some editing help, here are some excellent book editors I can recommend hiring [put names/contact info]. Or, if you're on a very tight budget, try **Grammarly** which is an online spelling/grammar checking system that I love. Congratulations on this achievement, once again!"

I love this approach because it allows me to say no—and protect my time, energy, and boundaries—while still being encouraging and helpful.

A few more examples: An acquaintance asks if they can meet up for coffee to pick my brain about writing, creativity, checklists, freelancing, launching a business, etc. I could say no—but then recommend my all-time favorite book for entrepreneurs.

Someone invites me to attend their birthday party, but it doesn't sound fun to me because I dislike big group activities and loud, noisy bars. I could decline the invite—but then suggest an alternative celebration: "I'd love to treat you to a special birthday brunch sometime this month, just you and I."

A friend asks if I can help them write an essay but I don't have time. I can say no—but then invite them to take my upcoming writing class at no charge, as a gift.

A friend asks me to pick them up from the airport on a hectic day when I don't have time to swing over. I could say no—but then send them a Lyft gift certificate as a surprise.

You get the idea. Try phrases like these:

- I can't do _____, but how about this instead…

- I won't be available for _____, but here's what I can suggest…

- I need to decline _____, but here's another option to consider…

- I'm not available for _____, but have you considered checking this out…

I wrote an eBook called *How to Say No* where I cover this topic more thoroughly and provide some email templates/suggestions for handling common requests.

This eBook is free and you'll find it here: alexandrafranzen.com/free-stuff/.

"I DON'T HAVE ACCESS TO A PRINTER. ALSO, I DON'T WANT TO WASTE PAPER. SO I HAVE TO KEEP MY CHECKLIST ON MY PHONE/ TABLET/COMPUTER/DIGITAL FORMAT. IS THAT OKAY?"

It's okay to use a digital checklist instead of a physical paper checklist…if you *really* must. However, digital is *not* ideal, and here's why.

Research from top institutions—including Harvard University—shows that our brains process information differently when we're reading something digital versus something physical.

With digital text (like a blog post, Kindle eBook, or digital checklist on your phone), your reading comprehension tends to be lower, you're more likely to become distracted, and you tend to retain less information.

On top of all that, you might experience eyestrain from the glow of the screen. And too much electronic light can disrupt your sleep cycles at night, which means you wake up feeling tired and grumpy. Not good.

Science aside, personally, I find that it just feels so much more *satisfying* to have a checklist I can hold in my hands. I love the feeling of taking a marker and putting a nice, big, fat checkmark next to completed items. I don't get that same feeling when I check things off a digital list. Maybe you do—if so, cool! But for me, a physical list always feels better.

(To be eco-conscious, of course, you can print on recycled paper and use both sides of the paper.)

> "I HATE BEING TOLD WHAT TO DO! I HATE RULES! I HATE RIGIDITY! I AM A FREE-SPIRITED GYPSY AND I VALUE FREEDOM AND SPONTANEITY! THE WHOLE IDEA OF MAKING A CHECKLIST JUST MAKES ME CRINGE."

I feel you! Freedom is one of my top values in life too. But I find that making a checklist actually brings *more* freedom into my life, not less.

By making a Daily Checklist, I become more focused and less distracted, more efficient with my time, and I can get important tasks done faster. This creates more free time for spontaneous experiences—like spontaneously texting a friend and saying, "I'm heading to the beach right now—want to meet me there?"

Also, I love including blank lines on my Daily Checklist to leave space for totally spontaneous ideas and activities that might arise during my day. With these blank lines, I am "planning ahead for spontaneity," which might seem like an oxymoron, but it really works for me.

> "WHEN I SIT DOWN TO MAKE A DAILY CHECKLIST—OR ANY CHECKLIST—I FEEL SO MENTALLY DISORGANIZED! I DON'T KNOW WHERE TO BEGIN! PLUS, MY KIDS/PETS/SPOUSE/CO-WORKERS KEEP INTERRUPTING ME. UGH."

The French phrase *mise en place* means "set up," "put in place," or "everything in its place."

If you wander into a kitchen, behind-the-scenes at a busy restaurant, you may hear a chef instructing her staff to "*mise it out!*"

This is a shorthand, kitchen-slang command that basically means: "Hey everyone! Listen up! We've got two hundred customers coming in tonight. Sharpen the knives. Wash the veggies. Wipe down the counter. Let's get everything clean, ready, and neatly set up—so we can throw down and get to work."

Before sitting down to make your next checklist, be sure to *mise it out*. Put everything in its place. Set yourself up for success. Gather the supplies that you need. Create a pleasant and organized environment. Close your office door and lock it. Remind your family that you're unavailable for the next thirty minutes (or however much time you need).

If it's too distracting at home (or the office), go elsewhere. A park bench. A coffee shop. Maybe a swanky hotel lobby. Somewhere you can exhale and think clearly.

Taking a few moments to *mise it out* can make a huge difference.

> "I FEEL CONFUSED ABOUT MY PURPOSE IN LIFE. I DON'T HAVE A CLEAR PHILOSOPHY, BELIEF SYSTEM, OR APPROACH TO LIFE. WHAT'S THE BEST WAY TO SPEND MY TIME? WHAT SHOULD I BE DOING EVERY DAY? I FEEL SO LOST."

Many people believe you "find" your purpose in life—like it's a shiny copper penny buried at the bottom of a well and then one day—hallelujah—you discover it!

I disagree. I don't think you "find" your purpose. I believe you "choose" your purpose—just like you choose which items to put onto your Daily Checklist, which items to put on your Seasonal Checklist, or anything else. You get to decide.

If you skipped it, I recommend that you go back and read "Chapter Four: The Big Question: How Do You Want to Spend Your Time?" In that chapter of this book, we explore some different ways to choose your approach to life. That chapter might be a good starting point for you.

You might also enjoy reading these two articles, which are posted on my website:

- "How to choose your purpose."
  http://bit.ly/choose-your-purpose
- "Read this if...you are anxiously searching for your life purpose."
  http://bit.ly/anxiously-searching

Ultimately, your approach to life (life purpose, mission, belief system, organizing principle, whatever you want to call it) can be as complex—or as simple—as you want. It might be just one or two words. It might be a short statement. Here are some statements that people have shared with me:

- Be kind.
- Spread love.
- Protect the earth.
- Make people laugh.
- Make beautiful things.
- Have orgasms and make art.
- Teach self-defense to 1,000 girls.
- Alleviate suffering in any way that I can.
- Leave the world in slightly better condition than I found it.

Lastly, if you're feeling really boggled and baffled and lost, talk to someone else. A mentor, elder figure in your community, spiritual leader, therapist, friend, or a group of friends all gathered around the dinner table. Oftentimes, talking it out with other people is the best way to gain the clarity you want.

> "I LOVE THE IDEA OF PUTTING 'MOMENTS' ON MY DAILY CHECKLIST—MOMENTS THAT ARE BEAUTIFUL AND NOURISHING. BUT THE REALITY IS, I RUN A BUSINESS, WORK FULL-TIME, HAVE FIVE KIDS, DON'T HAVE FREE TIME OR MUCH MONEY, ETC. I FEEL LIKE THERE'S ABSOLUTELY NO SPACE IN MY LIFE FOR THESE KINDS OF MOMENTS."

To quote my very wise mom, a woman who worked full-time while raising three kids:

> "WHEN YOU THINK YOU ABSOLUTELY CAN'T AFFORD TO TAKE A BREAK, THAT'S WHEN YOU NEED A BREAK MOST OF ALL."

Even if your life is outrageously busy—even if all you can spare is thirty seconds of deep breathing while you look out the window and admire the late-afternoon sky—take those thirty seconds of time for yourself. It's vitally important for your mental and physical wellbeing.

I am continually amazed by the power of *moments*. The tiniest moments—one minute to savor my coffee, two minutes to massage my forearms with lotion after a long day of typing, three minutes of meditation, a four-minute chat with my brother, telling him a hilarious story about something that happened earlier in the day—these tiny moments significantly improve how my day feels.

To quote my friend Megan DeBoer, a wonderful financial advisor with a beautiful perspective on life:

———————

"NOBODY WILL GIVE THIS TIME TO YOU.
YOU HAVE TO GIVE IT TO YOURSELF."

———————

Please give yourself whatever time you can give. Every minute helps. Every moment counts.

CLOSING THOUGHTS

The universe is vast and mysterious. Nobody knows exactly why we're here. There is no iron-clad document detailing the "correct way to live your life." You get to choose.

Choose an approach to life that feels right for you—and then stick with this approach as best you can.

Consistency feels good.

Create a Daily Checklist with a plan for your day—a plan that includes tasks you need to complete, and beautiful moments you want to experience. Don't cram your checklists with all tasks and no moments. The moments are vital.

Make other checklists, too—beautiful lists of things you want to experience this season, perhaps this year, and beyond. A checklist can be a visual reminder of the things you cherish most, much like a wedding ring or a tattoo with your child's name. A checklist can be a written symbol of the life you are currently living—and the life you aspire to build. A record of your intentions, accomplishments, and favorite memories, too.

Occasionally, take some time to think about death. Death has a funny way of rapidly clarifying how you wish to live.

If you had just twenty-four hours left to live, what would you do with your time? Who would you want to see? What words would you say to those people? What experiences would you want to have in your final hours? Whatever's on your "My Final 24" list, try to infuse some—or all—of these things into your regular everyday life, too. Because this could be the last day. Hopefully not. But maybe. So just in case, to quote my grandfather Selig who died long before I was born, "Never miss a sunset."

Above all, trust your hut (heart + gut).

Breathe.

Keep it simple.

Make a checklist.

ALEX

THIS IS MY DAILY CHECKLIST
FROM JUNE 13, 2019, THE DAY I
FINISHED WRITING THIS BOOK.

IT WAS AN AWESOME DAY.

CHECKLIST FOR
❧❧ JUNE 13, 2019 ❧❧

> "Slowly is the fastest way to get where you want to be."
> —André De Shields

✔ DRINK A BIG GLASS OF WATER. GOOD MORNING! IT'S GOING TO BE A GOOD DAY.

✔ TAKE A WALK DOWN TO SACK 'N SAVE. GET GROUND COFFEE AND HALF & HALF.

✔ MAKE A POT OF COFFEE

✔ MAKE YOUR BED

✔ TAI CHI MERIDIAN TAPPING EXERCISE

✔ DON'T CHECK YOUR EMAIL! FOCUS ON THE BOOK!

✔ LISTEN TO THE CHECKLIST BOOK PLAYLIST

✔ WRITE! WRITE! WRITE! FINISH THE BOOK! *Yesssssss!* ♥♥♥

✔ TAKE GEMMA TO CHALKS BEACH OR (AKAKA FALLS)

✔ ~~5 P.M. MEET UP WITH KATE AT NANILOO TO DISCUSS JUNE/JULY PROJECTS~~ *Resched for tmrw.*

✔ Get a salad at Vibe

✔ Text Brenda "Book is done!"

✔ Coordinate car repair time with Trey—tmrw at 11?

✔ 6:30 P.M. DRIVE GEMMA TO THE AIRPORT

✔ THROW SHEETS/CLOTHES INTO THE LAUNDRY MACHINE

✔ BREATHE AND REMEMBER THAT YOU'RE DOING A GREAT JOB

RECOMMENDED BOOKS,
WEBSITES, & OTHER
RESOURCES

A FEW BOOKS, WEBSITES, MUSIC PLAYLISTS,

OFFICE PRODUCTS, AND OTHER NICE THINGS TO

MAKE YOUR LIFE A LITTLE EASIER, CALMER, AND

MORE ORGANIZED.

BOOKS

If you enjoyed *The Checklist Book*, you might also enjoy reading:

- *Atomic Habits: An Easy & Proven Way to Build Good Habits & Break Bad Ones* by James Clear.

- *Die Empty: Unleash Your Best Work Every Day* by Todd Henry.

- *Eat That Frog!: 21 Great Ways to Stop Procrastinating and Get More Done in Less Time* by Brian Tracy.

- *Less: Accomplishing More by Doing Less* by Marc Lesser.

- *Life As a Daymaker: How to Change the World by Simply Making Someone's Day* by David Wagner.

- *How to Change Your Mind: What the New Science of Psychedelics Teaches Us About Consciousness, Dying, Addiction, Depression, and Transcendence* by Michael Pollan.

- *The Bullet Journal Method: Track the Past, Order the Present, Design the Future* by Ryder Carroll.

- *The Checklist Manifesto: How to Get Things Right* by Atul Gawande.

- *The Desire Map: A Guide to Creating Goals with Soul* by Danielle LaPorte.

- *The Life-Changing Magic of Tidying Up: The Japanese Art of Decluttering and Organizing* by Marie Kondo.

- *The Miracle Morning: The Not-So-Obvious Secret Guaranteed to Transform Your Life (Before 8AM)* by Hal Elrod.

- *The War of Art: Break Through the Blocks and Win Your Inner Creative Battles* by Steven Pressfield.

- *Zen To Done: The Ultimate Simple Productivity System* by Leo Babauta.

Here are some articles, podcasts, radio shows, and other interesting materials I came across while doing research for this book:

- *Air & Space.* "The Fourth Crew Member." airspacemag.com/space/the-fourth-crewmember-37046329/

- *Fast Company.* "Why Our Brains Love Lists And How To Make Better Ones." fastcompany.com/3040420/why-our-brains-love-lists-and-how-to-make-better-ones

- *Fast Company.* "You Won't Remember This Article, Or Anything Else You Read Online, Unless You Print It Out." fastcompany.com/3009366/you-wont-remember-this-article-or-anything-else-you-read-online-unless-you-pr

- *Mental Floss.* "5 Reasons Physical Books Might Be Better Than E-Books." mentalfloss.com/article/69380/5-reasons-physical-books-might-be-better-e-books

- *Press release: Tufts University.* "Training your brain to prefer healthy foods." eurekalert.org/pub_releases/2014-09/tuhs-tyb082714.php

- *National Public Radio (NPR).* "10 Reasons Why We Love Making Lists." npr.org/templates/story/story.php?storyId=101056819

- *National Public Radio (NPR).* "The Trick To Surviving A High-Stakes, High-Pressure Job? Try A Checklist." npr.org/2017/10/30/559996276/the-trick-to-surviving-a-high-stakes-high-pressure-job-try-a-checklist

- *Ted Talks.* "Why We All Need to Practice Emotional First Aid" with Guy Winch, Phd. ted.com/talks/guy_winch_the_case_for_emotional_hygiene

- *The Cut.* "A Neuroscientist on the Calming Powers of the To-Do List." thecut.com/2016/01/neuroscientist-really-wants-you-to-make-lists.html

- *The Guardian.* "The Psychology of the To-Do List—Why Your Brain Loves Ordered Tasks." theguardian.com/lifeandstyle/2017/may/10/the-psychology-of-the-to-do-list-why-your-brain-loves-ordered-tasks

- *The New Yorker.* "A List of Reasons Why Our Brains Love Lists." newyorker.com/tech/annals-of-technology/a-list-of-reasons-why-our-brains-love-lists

- *The Waiter's Pad.* "Danny Meyer." thewaiterspad.com/2017/03/10/danny-meyer/

- *Trello.* "How Checklists Train Your Brain To Be More Productive And Goal-Oriented." blog.trello.com/the-psychology-of-checklists-why-setting-small-goals-motivates-us-to-accomplish-bigger-things

- *Zen Habits.* "Purpose Your Day: Most Important Task (MIT)." zenhabits.net/purpose-your-day-most-important-task/

WONDERFUL CHECKLIST SUPPLIES

I love classic bulletin boards. Nothing fancy. Just a cork board with a simple wood frame. I usually get mine from Target and they're approximately two feet long, one and a half feet wide, and around $8 a piece. You can also find bulletin boards on Amazon or pretty much any office supply store. I also love Ubrand Fashion Push Pins from Target. Add a little sparkle to your boards! Just $3 for a pack of 54 pins.

To add a touch of luxury to your checklist-life, treat yourself to an A5 Stainless Steel Clipboard from NewBeer. On Amazon, it's about $16. I got one that's gold. It's so shiny, I can see my reflection in it! I feel very glamorous whenever I hold it.

I've tried many pens and markers, but my favorite is still the Original Sharpie Permanent Marker. A classic that never goes out of style! sharpie.com/markers

Throughout this book, I've mentioned that I really like to print out my Daily Checklist for the next day in the evening before I go to bed. That way, it's ready for me as soon as I wake up. Buying a printer is not as wildly expensive as you might think. Mine cost about $45. It's the Canon Pixma MG3620 All-In-One Printer/Scanner. It's not the fanciest printer on earth, but it gets the job done! I especially love the fact that it's bluetooth/wireless. You can get one on the Canon website (usa.canon.com) or Target or Amazon. (To be eco-conscious, of course, print on recycled paper whenever possible.)

If you're obsessed with notebooks, clipboards, journals, organizers, all kinds of office/art/crafting/paper goods, Paper Chase is your utopia. I wandered into one of their stores during a trip to London and then roamed around, glassy-eyed and mesmerized, for about two hours, stroking things and cooing, "Oooh, pretty." It's an amazing store for paper-lovers.
They ship worldwide. paperchase.com.

Bando (bando.com) is another really fun brand with colorful, charming writing supplies, folders, notebooks, stickers, tape, and more.

WEBSITES & OTHER RESOURCES

HIRE SOMEONE TO HELP OUT

Want to hire someone to help out with a household task, a work project, or pretty much anything at all?

From picking up groceries…to proofreading your essay…to designing a nice logo for your new business…to hand-delivering a surprise birthday gift to your friend who lives in another city... whatever you need, I can guarantee there's someone who'd love to do it today, for a very reasonable price! Search online and your wishes will be granted!

The following sites are great places to find a freelancer, errand runner, or any kind of part-time helper: Fiverr (fiverr.com), Hire My Mom (hiremymom.com), TaskRabbit (taskrabbit.com), The International Virtual Assistants Association (ivaa.org), and Upwork (upwork.com).

Looking to make some extra cash? Consider making a profile on one of the sites I just mentioned and you can start doing paid gigs—writing, editing, proofreading, graphic design, illustrating, cooking, driving around town, household repairs, cleaning, tutoring, whatever you want to do—on your own schedule, whenever you want! Nice!

BLOCK OUT DISTRACTIONS

Are there certain websites that feel very distracting, tempting, or maybe even emotionally triggering or harmful for you to see? Or perhaps, you'd like to block some sites so that your children can't see them? Try Blocksite. blocksite.co.

Is your inbox crammed with hundreds of email newsletters that you don't want? Use Unroll.me to unsubscribe from hundreds of newsletters—all at once. unroll.me.

Is your home (or office) cluttered with stuff you don't need? Old clothes, furniture, electronics, appliances, various distracting eye-sores that are impairing your ability to focus? Put everything into a box. Then go online (pickupplease.org) to schedule a free pick-up. A driver will swing by, pick up your unwanted goods, and donate them to American Veterans who need them. They'll even leave behind a tax-deduction receipt for you. How cool is that?

Want to block out distracting sounds from your environment? I love my Bose QuietComfort 35 Wireless Bluetooth Headphones. You can use them to create a soothing white-noise experience—and block out your noisy neighbors who love to hold their ukulele band practice at 11 p.m. at night, for instance. These Bose headphones are also great for listening to music, podcasts, or audiobooks. Excellent sound quality. No annoying wires. These headphones are expensive (around $300), but I've used mine several hours per day, practically every single day of my life, for many years in a row—so for me, it's been a totally worthwhile investment. Search on amazon.com or bose.com to find these.

MUSIC TO HELP YOU FOCUS

Some people prefer working in complete silence. Other people (like me!) find that they're able to focus better with some music or ambient sound in the background.

I've created hundreds of music playlists on Spotify, a music streaming service that costs $9.99 per month for the premium membership, which includes unlimited music and zero ads/commercials. Some of my Spotify playlists are very soothing while others are energizing. Some have lyrics and some don't. You can find all of my favorite music playlists here: open.spotify.com/user/alex_franzen

Here's a playlist with the music I listened to while writing this book: http://bit.ly/checklist-book

I also love Coffitivity (coffitivity.com), a website that recreates the sound of a cheerful, bustling coffee shop. People murmuring in the distance, steam from an espresso machine, gentle clattering and footsteps. It's weirdly soothing and hypnotic! You can play it while you're at home—and you'll be instantly transported to a café.

While I don't use it personally, I have friends who absolutely love Focus@Will (focusatwill.com). This is a music streaming service developed by neuroscientists. All the music is carefully selected to help you "focus, reduce distractions, maintain your productivity and retain information when working, studying, writing and reading."

MORE RESOURCES

I'm always discovering new books, websites, music playlists, products, and other resources that I love.

If you'd like to receive occasional updates from me (new discoveries, inspiring stories, announcements, etc.), please sign up for my newsletter: alexandrafranzen.com/newsletter.

For downloadable checklist templates, please visit: alexandrafranzen.com/checklists.

Thank you!

EVERY MINUTE
HELPS.
EVERY MOMENT
COUNTS.

ACKNOWLEDGMENTS

Creating a book is always a team effort. I have so many people to thank, including...

My mom, dad, sister, brother, and sister-in-law. You are infinitely precious to me. Our wacky family-unit is my rock of emotional support. You make me laugh harder than anyone else on the planet. I love you. PS: Whale sounds.

Kate Lyness. My business manager, event coordinator, doer-of-all-things, and more importantly, my dear friend. You make my life easier and more beautiful in one thousand different ways. Thank you.

Melissa Cassera. Friiiiiiiend! Thank you for always texting to check in and see, "How is your heart doing today?" I love our hundreds of conversations on self-esteem, confidence, organizing projects, writing, tiny pumpkins, peanut butter, and more. So much of your spirit is imbued in this book.

Brenda Knight. Thank you for encouraging me to write this book—and for giving me a wonderful *you-can-do-this* pep talk when my self-confidence was drooping. You've been a huge champion of my writing for years. I'm forever indebted to you.

Everyone at Mango Publishing. Elina Diaz, Jessica Faroy, MJ Fievre, Liz Hong, Shawn Hoult, Mitchell Kaplan, Jermaine Lau, Morgane Leoni, Christina McCall, Chris McKenney, Scott McKenney, Robin Miller, Roberto Nuñez, Hannah Jorstad Paulsen, Yaddyra Peralta, Alina Perrin, Giulia Scarnecchia, Julian Segal, Merritt Smail, Natasha Vera, Laura Victor, Hugo Villabona, and Ronchon Villaester. Thank you for bringing this book into being—and thank you for collaborating with me to create The Tiny Press, too. You're all incredibly hardworking, patient, supportive, and just all-around delightful.

Everyone at Yoga Centered in Hilo, Hawaii. The studio has been my second-home and my sanctuary. Without daily yoga and meditation classes, I would truly lose my marbles. Molly, Lauren, Donna, Elisha, Amanda, all the ladies and gentlemen at YC, all of you are wonderful. Thank you for welcoming me into your community with open arms.

Gemma Stone, Ryan Brown, Dr. Sasha Heinz, Dr. Suzanne Gelb, Susan Hyatt, Sarah Von Bargen, Megan DeBoer, and many other psychologists, therapists, counselors, and coaches who have influenced the way I think about human minds and how they work.

A thousand other people that I'm forgetting. Thank you. For everything.

THANK

YOU

ABOUT THE AUTHOR

Alexandra Franzen is an author, entrepreneur, and proud "checklist freak."

She has written articles for numerous print and online publications, including *Time*, *Forbes*, *Newsweek*, *The Huffington Post*, *The Muse*, and *Lifehacker*. Her work has been mentioned in *The Los Angeles Times*, *The New York Times Small Business Blog*, *The Atlantic*, *USA Today*, and *Inc.*

She writes about a wide range of topics, from falling in love to coping with death. She's best known for her short essays on how to simplify daily life, set meaningful goals, spend our time thoughtfully, and overcome challenging experiences.

Her books include *You're Going to Survive*, a collection of true stories and advice on how to survive painful experiences in your career, *50 Ways to Say You're Awesome*, a book about the power of gratitude, and *So This Is the End: A Love Story*, a novel about a woman with exactly one day to live.

Alexandra is the founder of The Tiny Press, a publishing imprint specializing in short books that are around one hundred pages long. Big ideas in small packages.

She also works as a writer-for-hire, helping clients complete all kinds of writing/storytelling/media projects, including book proposals, websites, podcasts, marketing campaigns, and more.

She lives in a house with an entire wall that's covered in bulletin boards and checklists. To learn more, visit her website: alexandrafranzen.com.